For my wife,

Without you, I never would have finished the trip.

But I would have finished writing the book a lot faster.

CONTENTS

Contents

Foreward

One quarter of a year does not seem like that long of a time. But September through December of 2012 will be burned into my memory forever. I read somewhere that the reason time appears to move quicker as we age is partially because of our ability to take comfort in routine. I believe this to be true. During those months, my friend Shaun and I had just one true constant—pedaling forward. A concentration of new experiences and adventure does change your perception of time. Three months felt like a year to us. We were living outside of the norm, which allowed us to slow down and soak in every moment, good and bad. I can remember more details about those several months, almost a decade ago, than details from the past week.

Shaun originally approached me with the idea to cycle across the country. I thought it was a big idea that might fizzle out, but it kept popping up in our conversations until it became a fact that we were going to carry through with our plan. Eventually, dates and details started to line up and point to a moment in time as the opportunity we were hoping for. We seized that opportunity and it turned into a sizable life experience that neither of us truly expected. I'm grateful for our trip and I will cherish those experiences and bonds that we made with the people along the way.

On this one particular night, there was a new moon. We were in the middle of nowhere, far away from civilization. I stood in the dark, astonished as I watched my best friend drag his bike off of the road sideways, over and through desert shrubs, with a string of obscenities following him into the night. I remember thinking, "Does he know that bikes have wheels and can roll?" Once he was no longer illuminated by the light attached to my handlebars, I figured it was best to follow him.

Shaun was angry, a very uncommon spectacle. We'd already had to fix another flat tire that night, and it was cold —colder than usual. We both lacked appropriate sub-freezing apparel, but I was willing to put up with the temperature just to get farther down the road. We were (and still are) polar opposites when it came to riding temps, so I knew that Shaun was miserable. His gloves were not protecting against the extra wind chill, inevitably becoming the tipping point of his frustration. When I caught up to him, he told me that he was not going any farther that night, so we set up camp right there.

Perhaps I was pushing too hard. At this point in the trip, I was still hanging onto schedules. However, one compelling reason to kick it into big gear was the cold weather. It was only going to get worse if we didn't outrun it and move farther south. Another reason, although incredibly selfish, was that I wanted to be at a certain place for my birthday. But more on that later. As you'll see in this book, tensions ran high at times but we managed through okay and got to the other side (literally) with a better understanding of each other and a better understanding of ourselves.

My memories of our trip will stay with me, but I am not always able to put them all into words. I think it is amazing that Shaun was able to document these experiences and share the story of our trip from his perspective. I hope you will see that his narrative is so much more than a story about two friends cycling from Washington to Florida.

Looking back, we were still young and I think both of us were searching for something and trying to figure things out before beginning our next chapters in life. Did I find what I was looking for? At the end of our trip, I would have told you no. I foolishly thought that somewhere along the way, a master life plan or even a next step would somehow be presented to me. I see now that instead, I have this incredible accomplishment that I can reflect upon. I can

Foreward

draw from those experiences and use them to help me navigate through whatever path I'm currently pursuing.

If you have read this far, may I offer this to you: There are many reasons why we find it hard to escape from our routines. I understand that family, work, and obligations are a reality for most. I was fortunate and privileged to be able to leave everything behind for three months. But if you crave adventure and exploration, keep searching for opportunities and do not immediately dismiss them. These opportunities, as small as they may be, can shape you and better you. Perhaps camping for a weekend or even going on a nature hike can soothe your soul. Find what speaks to you and makes you a human.

– Be kind to one another,
Geoffrey Buell

CAST OF CHARACTERS

As soon as I learned of the novelists' practice of presenting a story's characters before the book begins, I immediately fell in love with it. And so I begin with such a list here. (However convenient the introduction is in literature, though, I loathe a long introduction in movies. If by some chance every bit of text has been erased from the earth, yet my book survives, and someone wants to make a movie, do not under any circumstances have a long introduction to the ill-fated film.)

Ashley and Dave - Our first hosts in Seattle, WA

Dale - Resembled a *King of the Hill* character

Fixed Gear Guy - A fleeting legend on the West Coast

Garrett - The kind soul that gave us food in Texas

Geoff Buell - Best friend of Shaun

German Paul - Sage cyclist

Hannah - Ex-girlfriend of Shaun

Ingrid Voelkel and Guilford Jones - Creators of La Loma del

Chivo

Jessie - Red-headed cyclist from Seattle, WA

Kaitlyn - Girlfriend of Shaun

Kenny - Anderson University roommate

Liz - Actress from *Swamp People*

Luap - Mustachioed hipster

Mae and Elwood - Austin, TX hosts who let strangers into their house

Matt - Cyclist who smoked a cigarette after every big hill

Mike - Credit card cycle tourist we met in Astoria, OR

Mike - Builder at del Chivo

Paul - Wanted to push a car across the United States

Randy - Father of Shaun

Rhea - Quirky woman from Colorado

Richie and Lilly - Our fantastic, genuine hosts in El Paso, TX

Scott - Host in Tacoma, WA

Scott's roommate - Giver of whiskey and stories

Steve and Linda - Cycled across America as a family of five

Tom - Mohawk-wearing wild man we met in the desert

Yaris - English cycle tourist who used only a compass

Introduction

Everyone has a story that needs to be shared. On my bicycle tour across America, everyone I met had a story they wanted to tell me, and I did my best to listen intently. Long before I started pedaling, I learned that investing in people is what life is all about. It took years of practice, but I finally started to take action by sharing stories, which became a powerful way to connect with fellow cyclists and adventure-enthusiasts on my trip. Whether sitting around a fire while getting pelted by ice, or eating low-country boil in a stranger's house, I listened to every word of every person I met, honored that I had the opportunity to talk with them. I hope my memoir will do their kindness, and their stories, justice.

Introduction

I am reaching deep into my thoughts and pull out the smallest details from memories years ago. I imagine lines on my friends' faces where wrinkles could have been. I know the creases exist, but I can't remember where, so I fill in the blanks. I pay attention to the smallest details; so much so, it sometimes blurs the big picture.

It's been nearly nine years since my best friend, Geoff Buell, and I started our bicycle ride across America. The intricacies of that trip paint the big picture, and as much as possible, I will try to paint what actually happened. Even if the truth is too far gone and the detailed memories faded, I hope to do justice to what happened. I want to tell everyone about the kindness and compassion that we met on the road, which tempered my growing resentment toward people in my life. That was my real lesson learned, wrapped in the subtleties of an adventure that changed our lives forever. Day after day, we made these stories beside the white line.

A Deal Is A Deal

Our senior year of high school started in 2005, and in keeping with the truest sense of that year's style, I had curly blonde hair down to my shoulders, I wore a puka shell necklace and a letterman's jacket nearly every day, and my footwear alternated between black Converse and tan, steel-toe boots. I always sat with the same group of friends, who were all athletes, but most of them runners. Geoff Buell was my best friend on the cross-country team. His bushy pony-tail and my blonde afro made for quite the distinguishable pair running around upstate South Carolina. We were al-ways pushing each other to go faster and be stronger. Every year we lifted weights in the summer, and we ran in the winter. It made for a cyclical high school experience, but we loved it, and we were good at it.

A Deal is a Deal

As our senior year came to an end, we got the idea to do a triathlon together. I had gotten injured weightlifting and needed a reprieve from the monotony of picking things up and putting them down. A triathlon seemed the best way to dive further into the endurance realm while allowing my weight lifting injuries to heal up. We talked about the idea in passing after I watched the Ironman World Championships on TV one day, but the more I researched it, the more I got the itch to try it.

One day at lunch, I was eating my daily chicken patty sandwich when I asked Geoff if he wanted to sign up for a sprint triathlon. Never one to dive into anything haphazardly, he seemed skeptical at first. It took an evening of watching some tear-jerking, inspirational Ironman clips, and he was down to try it.

The first day of training went about as well as could be expected. I swam a couple of laps in a neighborhood pool, rode my BMX bike a couple of miles, and finally ran a mile to the end of my neighborhood and back. I was exhausted, but worse than that, my knees were killing me. I quickly learned two lessons that day, the more obvious of which was that I was out of shape, and that a BMX bicycle is not the ideal bike for distance riding. I asked my parents for an actual road bike, and they said, "You can use the old mountain bike that's out in the garage. If you can complete a triathlon on that, we'll buy you a road bike for your next one." I cringed at the idea, imagining the rusted bike in the garage covered in spider webs. The purple paint on the bike had turned pink from sun bleaching, and quarter-sized flakes of presumably lead paint were chipping off. The gears were rusty, and the tires were dry-rotted and flat. It was not in perfect shape, but I also couldn't afford a bike, so I had to make it work.

Geoff and I graduated high school that spring, and the triathlon training immediately kicked up a notch. The first day of official training, I managed to replace the dry-rotted tires with the cheapest tires I could find, which happened to be heavy, knobby mountain-bike tires. I sprayed some WD-40 on the gears, and off I went. *The rust will add some resistance training and eventually wear off.... I hope.* We were riding every day, running every other day, and swimming whenever we could. The weight room was still a favorite spot of ours too, so we threw that in nearly every day as well. We felt unstoppable.

Our first sprint triathlon was scheduled for 7 AM on a Saturday, just four months after we'd started training. Every "how to do a triathlon" video we'd watched said to be there at least an hour early to set up, which made sense. However, the night before race day, we realized we had absolutely no idea how to set up properly or how long it would take, so we decided to get there two hours early, just to make sure. We left the house around 4 AM and got pulled over by the police around 4:20 AM. *I guess two guys in a truck, with disassembled, rusty bicycles stacked up in the back, was not a good look*. I'll admit my newly acquired mohawk probably didn't help anything, but we explained our situation and the officer let us go.

We made it to the staging area by 5 AM. There were a handful of bikes set up in the transition area and I could already tell that I was out of my league. There were bikes that looked like they came from Lance Armstrong's private reserve, people with calves the size of grapefruits, and even aerodynamically efficient handlebars that cost more than my entire bike. I did my best to stay positive and focused on running my race, but it wasn't easy.

We set up our bikes, staged our shoes and jerseys neatly in front, and thought of a solution to every scenario that could go wrong in the transition. Seven o'clock came quickly. I heard the whistle for the first wave of swimmers to start and a strong panic came over me, thinking I had missed the start. I sprinted to the pool.

It was a staggered start, which meant every ten seconds, they would let the next two racers begin. Luckily, Geoff and I were not supposed to swim until 7:30. Everyone waiting their turn sat on the edge of the pool with their feet dangling in the water, doing an awkward shuffle down the wall as more swimmers took off.

I was next. I dipped my body into the cold water and held onto the edge, ready to explode off the wall. I was slated to start one heat before Geoff. The whistle blew, and I kicked off the wall as hard as I could to get away from the stranger that began with me. I got a few strokes into the swim before I heard the next whistle, signaling Geoff to start. We were racing.

I felt phenomenal in the pool, like it was my natural habitat. I dodged my competitors' flailing arms and legs as I passed them. I finished the swim and transitioned to the bike and, well, that went about as smoothly as I had expected. It was like watching a sex scene with parents: awkward, it took too long, and I wanted to leave. It took so long for me to get my cycling jersey on that I eventually asked someone for help pulling my shirt down. *Well, that's embarrassing.* Geoff made up the nearly two-minute time difference between us and caught me in the transition area. "It's only right to start the bike portion together," I told Geoff, justifying the embarrassing shirt incident.

The bike ride was supposed to be a blazing fast fifteen miles, but on a rusted out mountain bike, it took every ounce of energy I had just to make the bike move. My legs were pumped with blood and lactic acid at the end of the bike stage, but having trained for the bike-to-run transition multiple times, I thought I was ready. I knew that it was supposed to feel like my legs weren't working when I started the run.

Right on cue, I got off the bike and my legs felt broken. *This is normal. Just move them forward.* My running form looked like I was a clown on stilts, but at least I was heading toward the finish line. The 5K run wasn't easy, but I had the endurance base from my years of running cross country to make it through. *I should have trained for the run more.*

I crossed the finish line in a full sprint, or at least I used whatever energy I could muster up to run semi-fast. I remember wanting to collapse afterward, but I was so elated from having finished the race that I managed to wander around to find my family and Geoff. *Geoff? Wait, where did Geoff go?* I had lost him at some point during the race, or he had lost me, but either way, I had no idea where he had gone.

It turned out he had passed me on the run and beat me by a few minutes, but I didn't care because we had finished. Finishing a long-distance event is a huge accomplishment and falls into one of the two trains of thought when it comes to endurance challenges: completing the event or winning the event. Completing the challenge has always been the most significant part for Geoff and me, hands down, but now that the sprint triathlon was under our belts, it was time to go further and tackle something harder. *I might as well use the new bike I just earned.*

Graduation Day

"So how far do you actually think you will make it?"
– Dad

High school was over. Finally, the weight of the world was off my shoulders. I could do whatever I wanted, they said. The world was mine, they said. As most people already know, they lied. I spent two years at a technical college because my dad said, "Go to school or join the military." *Oh, maybe after this I'll be free.* I transferred to Anderson University because I enjoyed chasing women. *If I was going to be in school, I was going to have fun.* As foolhardy as that sounds, I transferred colleges again to Winthrop University because I enjoyed chasing a particular woman. It didn't work out between us, but I'll get to that story later. When all was said and done, I graduated with a four-year degree and dating an entirely different woman—neither one I had planned for, and only one I appreciated. *Degrees are overrated.*

However overrated and overpriced a degree may be, the time spent at college helped me learn one crucial lesson: do whatever you want and do it with passion. I'm in full support of formal education if the student is wanting to learn, but forcing people to attend an overpriced four-year university to get a piece of paper that says, "I'm qualified to work now" is ludicrous. It was a lesson I learned at the cost of a mountain of student loan debt. *OK. I'm off my soapbox. I promise.*

Graduation day at Winthrop University. It was supposed to be 95 degrees outside, and I was instructed to wear pants and a collared shirt underneath my black graduation gown. *Nope, today is my day.* I donned black shorts, a black button-up shirt, a skinny red tie, and red suspenders with black canvas shoes. I was fashionable and not dying of heat exhaustion, even though my outfit was all black. I managed to catch a couple of weird stares as I walked across the stage to grab my diploma, most likely because I looked nude underneath my gown, and mooning the audience was not out of the realm of possibility for me. I shrugged off the stares, took the diploma, and shook someone's hand. I had graduated. Freedom had finally arrived on an 8½" by 11" sheet of paper. I felt both a deep sense of relief and excitement, but it all gave way to hunger, as most things in my life do, and all I could think about was the graduation party and food.

Amen and hallelujah, I made it to lunch at my aunt's house. Everyone there seemed proud of me for graduating. I was happy enough that I hadn't passed out from hunger while posing for pictures after the ceremony. Somewhere in the chaos of nachos and dip being funneled into my mouth, I faced questions like, "So what's next?" and "Do you have a job lined up?" The interrogation made me cringe because I didn't have an answer that would earn their approval. I wanted so desperately for a nacho to stab me in the tongue and prevent the words from leaving my lips.

"I'm going to work at a camp for the summer, save up a bit, then ride my bike across America," I said with a confident appearance, yet trembling insides. Their smiles turned to looks of concern. I wasn't sure what their reaction would be. Maybe I'd just tell them what route I'd be taking, and it would blow over, which could have happened had it not been my graduation day with all of the attention on me. If I were a military man, that was the moment I'd be preparing for mortar fire, taking cover and grasping the cross around my neck. This was the pivotal moment where it all came down to dodging bullets.

I hadn't thought of many of their questions about the trip, so in that way, the barrage of questions was really a bit helpful. While mentally taking note of every unanswered question, I blundered through the rest, stuttering and digging for quick, clever answers. *Bullet dodged.* I felt pressured, as though if I didn't answer each question correctly, my dreams of riding would disappear before I even went to sleep. My stomach began twisting, from tension or nachos; there was no telling which. Some family members seemed genuinely interested in my plans. Others asked questions with a pointed intent of cornering me into the idea that cycling across America was impossible.

My motivation took a punch in the jaw when my dad asked if I would carry a firearm. With my best interests in mind, he asked how I'd defend myself when I was attacked. *Not if, but when. Are you kidding me?!*

The idea of a small .22 caliber handgun nestled comfortably in my saddlebag flittered around for a bit, but ultimately I decided against it. The trip was supposed to be about who America was, and if I took a gun, then it showed I had made up my mind without ever asking, "Who are you, America?"

After a moment of dead conversation, my father broke the tension with, "So how far do you actually think you will make it?" Never in my life had I been so thunderstruck by someone's doubt. Albeit, it was a simple query about my resolve to finish the trip, but it shook me.

Questions have changed history, time and time again. The world has always been changed by ordinary people asking questions. Why did the apple fall, or is the moon literally made of cheese? And why, up until that point, had I never paid homage to the power of a question? *How far will I make it?* I sat back in my chair, answering on autopilot, "The whole way," while my mind spun. It was as though the world were shaking back and forth too quickly to discern the image. I quit trying to focus. My hearing went muffled like a blanket was thrown over my eardrums. I quit trying to listen. My heart was pounding so hard I could feel the erratic pulse thumping on the side of my neck. Every sense dulled as my focus dialed in on my right hand, shaking, just enough for only me to notice. *Of course I'll make it the whole way.* If failure had been an option, my dad's pessimistic question had made it an impossibility. *My pride will carry me.*

I do not remember the rest of the party. The question, and my dad's doubt, reverberated inside my head for months.

Counselor Hunt

Sweat dripped over my eyebrow, trying desperately to land in the corner of my eye. I blinked hard to make the droplet slide down my cheek. I dared not move my body, for this was more perilous than a war zone. It was Counselor Hunt at summer camp.

The summer before my trip, I landed a job at a camp in York, South Carolina. Every week, new campers came for a fun-filled, tradition-packed camp experience. That particular day, four weeks away from departing on my trip, was the first time I could participate in the evening activity affectionately named Counselor Hunt. This momentous occasion was a weekly event where the campers chased down the counselors in a massive game of hide and seek. Why did the campers put so much passion and sweat into chasing down counselors? The campers' coveted reward for catching the counselors was to make the counselors walk the plank, pirate style, off the diving board and into the pool. In my mind, this game was no game at all.

The counselors always got a five-minute head start to run and hide from the campers. *I don't need it.* I ran and hid nearby in a foolproof spot, facedown in a ditch. I was fully dressed in black and green attire, submerged in a pile of underbrush, and lying as still as possible. *God I hope this isn't poison ivy.* I took silent breaths, just a few yards away from where the enemies (or "campers" as some called them) were impatiently waiting to start their chase. *This week, my first week, I will not be caught. I will outrun all two hundred campers, or die trying.*

There'd been a windstorm the night before, making the ground green with torn leaves. Branches littered the surrounding area. The trails were damp from the rain runoff; although, the humidity in South Carolina was always thick, leaving the trails forever damp. Clear skies, wet leaves, ninety-five percent humidity, and I was dressed in long sleeves during the middle of the summer.

I waited silently for the camp's dinner bell to ring, signaling the start of the hunt. My breathing made my chest rise and fall, crinkling the leaves. I didn't want anything to give away my position, so I raised my stomach off the ground and took breaths using my diaphragm. That way, my stomach, instead of my chest, rose and fell, without making a sound. My ears were tuned to everything. I heard drops of water falling off the leaves overhead. The bell rang. The enemy screamed orders to each other.

"Run this way!"

"No, they're over here!"

The younger campers ran right past me, nearly tripping over my feet. Once they passed, I could hear the almost militant older campers barking strategic orders at each other to survey the perimeter. *Here we go.*

I turned my head, searching for a glimpse of the enemy trying to hunt me out of my safe home in the ditch. *Of course, Mr. Track Star.* He'd told me earlier that day that he ran 40 meters in 4.4 seconds. I've always been a distance guy, so I'm not fast in short bursts. *I'm about as good at sprinting as I am cooking, which could explain why I'm hungry all the time. Food!? I'm thinking about food right now? Shut up and focus!*

The freshly applied mud on my face was still dripping wet. My right ear pressed to the ground. I could hear my heartbeat or the thunder of campers running; they sounded the same. I moved my arms by my side, positioning my palms down and elbows up. *No one sees me.* My best chance to escape was a surprise explosion out of the ditch to a spot where I could evade capture, a couple of hundred yards down the trail near the outdoor activities area. *I could hide near the basketball court. I can outrun them, I hope.* I waited for Mr. Track Star to get as far away as possible, but it wasn't happening. *Did we just make eye contact? He saw me! No, he didn't. He is still looking around. There is no way he saw me.* Ten meters away. *Stay calm.* Eight meters. *I need to move now.* Six meters. He made eye contact again.

I exploded out of the ditch, running toward the pool house with everything I had. *Long sleeves were a bad idea.* I sprinted down the trail, dodging stumps, roots, and the branches that had fallen the previous night. The muddy trail made it difficult to run, but that was to my advantage. I was used to the wet trails. I made a hard left just after the basketball court to try and lose Mr. Track Star in the woods. The mud was slowing him down. Running as hard as I could toward a fork in the trail, I waited until the last second to decide which path I was going to take. I sprinted down the trail to the right.

My sweat made the mud on my face heavy. The green, wet leaves on the trail made each step dangerous. *I should stop. I'm getting tired.* Mr. Track Star was gaining on me. The trail took a hard left. I didn't slow. A tree had fallen the night before. Green and alive, it blocked the entire trail. *This is it. I can lose him here.* I jumped the tree in classic high school hurdler fashion. Right leg forward, left leg back and bent. *I make this look good.* In a slow-motion sequence, I saw the tree going under me. Fast forward to a super-lightning-fast sequence—I did not see the second tree behind it. *Shit.* I tried to stretch just a little further to clear it. *Not good, not good.* I leaned forward to make sure my feet didn't catch the tree and make me go tumbling down the trail.

Right foot touched the ground.

Pop.

It was not a loud sound when I landed, just a quiet pop.

I yelled. It was not quite a vocal-cord-shattering scream, but loud enough to let everyone know that my leg was not okay. *I'm four weeks away from the trip. My leg has to be okay.* I tried to stand to walk it off, but my knee buckled out from under me. I fell back into the mud as tears welled up, not because of the pain but because I needed my legs to work in four weeks when I started to ride a bicycle across America. My number one fear was also trying to take over, but I'll get to that later. Luckily Mr. Track Star was there. I sent him to get help. *Clearly, I'm not going anywhere.*

After hobbling back to the main office lodge with the help of some friends, I got ice for my leg and couldn't help but feel this overwhelming sense that my adventure was over before it started. Self-pity and rage began to eat away at any hope I had. I didn't mind the pain; it was the inability to use my leg that scared me. I was on a timeline that wasn't long enough for it to heal.

Interrupting my pity party, one of the campers, a pre-teen female, slammed open the door and came running into the office shrieking and crying. Counselors followed her, unsuccessfully consoling her while trying to figure out what to do.

I rapidly sat up on the couch. "What happened?!"

"She laid on top of a yellow jacket nest! What should we do?"

"Come over here so I can see. Where are you stung?" I asked the girl. She could barely stop screaming long enough to answer me, but she began pointing everywhere.

"We need to get female counselors here, and we need to get these stingers out of her," I told the fastest guy in the room, and he bolted out the door.

I did my best to calm her. While I tried to pull a stinger out of her leg, she let out the shrillest scream I've ever heard and began swatting at her back. *The bees are still in her clothes.*

The female counselors arrived, and I told them to undress her and make sure the bees were gone. They went behind a three-fourth wall and took her shirt off. I saw at least six bees fly up to the ceiling. *She's still under attack.*

It took thirty minutes to find and remove all thirteen stingers, and to treat at least a dozen more stings. She was okay after some Benadryl and ice cream, but I suddenly didn't care about my leg anymore.

Packing Up

It took three weeks of intense physical therapy, but I got my leg movable again, just in time to start packing my bags. My summer at camp was over. I only had two weeks before Geoff and I flew to Seattle to start pedaling. We had always challenged each other, whether in the gym or on the track, but this trip stemmed from a different place. We weren't trying to one-up each other, but instead we were almost asking for help.

One day during lunch in 2004, Geoff had casually asked, "Do you want to hike the Appalachian Trail with me?"

"Sure, as long as we cycle across America too," I said, acting as if both were a walk in the park. The request for a teammate had been made under the guise of a thrown gauntlet. It took us eight years to prepare our lives, but we were two weeks away from adventure number one: cycling across America.

I had done my best to save money working at camp, where I'd spent zero on food and rent, but minimum wage was still minimum wage, and I was not financially ready to leave. As I watched heartfelt documentaries and read motivating stories about other people's endurance challenges, I became transfixed. I was so focused on getting in shape, studying maps, having the right equipment, and building up enough motivation that I had no mental room left to worry about finances. However, I did notice a common theme among many of the adventurers I studied: they had sponsorship. Boom, the answer to all my problems was staring right at me in the big, bold logos branded across almost every adventurer I watched in those documentaries.

Working every day, I threw my story out for the world to hear it. The first step I took was to start a blog. *Surely that will get some attention.* I then contacted bike companies, food companies, and various media outlets, in an attempt to become a branded cycle tourist. I waited by my computer day and night, but got only an overwhelming response of crickets. Granted, I could have done a better job of reaching out. I mean, emailing the "contact" button on a website isn't exactly a hard-charging method of getting sponsors. However, my blog got a ton of exposure, with over a thousand views in just the first hour! I knew people were excited for me, but I had no idea it would take off like that. I gained more momentum when many of my friends and family donated money to help out. The experience was a powerful rallying cry of encouragement that I'd never expected. I sat back in my computer chair one night with tears of gratitude dropping onto my keyboard, knowing that I would be forever indebted. I could never have started without my friends' and family's help.

The financial deposits trickling in kept me moving forward, even though I knew they wouldn't cover the total cost of the trip. Some would call that blind faith, but I prefer to look at it like a bull looks at a red cape. With no idea what's behind the waving red fabric, he charges and never looks back. I've never seen a bull stop to think about the consequences, so I wouldn't either. I had a goal and would not let financial fear hold me back. *Yes, the bull eventually dies, but they don't call it bull-headed for nothing.*

While I was struggling to raise funds for the trip, Geoff was doing a much better job preparing. He had graduated college with a degree in illustration, and was doing freelance work while working at a bike shop. Many of his coworkers were semi-pro cyclists, so Geoff had no shortage of fantastic training partners. He also had a phenomenal discount on his cycling gear, so he had the best equipment and was better prepared physically and financially.

Geoff came over a few days before we were scheduled to leave, to lay out and inspect all of our gear. My house

looked like a bomb went off in a bike shop. There were
tubes, tires, pumps, water bottles, hats, saddles (another
name for bike seats), bike locks, bike boxes, shoes,
notebooks, panniers, first aid kits, clothes, sleeping bags, pil-
lows, toiletries, helmets, waterproof bags, cookware, and
even books strewn about my house, and that's the shortlist.
We essentially had everything we needed to survive any disaster that could maybe, possibly have a slight chance of happening. Still, we checked and rechecked everything. It took
us the better part of two days to disassemble the bikes,
check out every component, brainstorm any possible instance in which we might need a particular tool, then debate
for an hour if we deemed it essential or not. We were packing our entire lives into a few boxes, and I wanted to make
sure we had what we needed. I knew I was going to live off
my bike for months, and clinging to my gear had slowly become my security blanket.

We ended up with five boxes in total: a box for each
bike, a box for my luggage, a box for Geoff's luggage, and
then a box for the bike trailer that also housed an assortment of other gear. We shoved everything else that wouldn't
fit in our luggage boxes into the trailer box, which we
deemed "the random box." I even stuffed a full-sized pillow
in there for some semblance of comfort, knowing I would be
sleeping on the ground for months.

The textured wall of the apartment felt good against
my back as I stared at the five boxes. The reality of the whole

thing started to set in. We were going to manually move our bodies across the United States of America.

What if I don't make it? The question kept slamming around in my mind the entire night before we left, keeping sleep far away and welcoming doubt like a cozy blanket. *I can't get sponsors, Dad doesn't think I'll make it, I don't have enough money, and my knee is not 100 percent.* I knew full well that it was not a solid plan, but that had never stopped me before. I just needed to sleep and wake up. That's all I needed to do right then. For everything else, I would take it one pedal stroke at a time. *Sleep and wake up. Sleep first, then wake up. Sleep.*

Sleep finally came. Hard.

Airport

Turn off alarm. Open eyelids. Move covers off of body.
Fundamental, deliberate instructions that kept my body
moving toward the airport. It was time to leave the apartment and fly to the starting line. Time to say goodbye to
Kaitlyn. *Hug her. Kiss her. Put bag by front door.* I kept
putting the most uncomplicated thoughts at the forefront of
my mind because I didn't want to say goodbye. Kaitlyn was
my girlfriend of eight months and had been incredibly sup-
portive. We even accidentally moved in together because I
had nowhere else to keep my stuff while I was riding. She
was a 5' 7" brunette dance major with short hair and the
most excellent laugh. I knew I was going to have challenges
coming up, but saying goodbye to her was going to be chal-

lenge number one, and the real starting line of the adventure. So I put the thought of leaving in the back of my mind. I needed to keep moving forward.

Geoff was already packed and drinking coffee by the time I finished brushing my teeth. *Geez, this guy loves waking up early.* I rushed around the apartment all day, gathering my boxes, drinking coffee, and rechecking to see if I was leaving anything. In the chaos of compulsively making sure every piece of gear was accounted for, I lost track of the time. We didn't actually leave the apartment until four in the afternoon, which left no margin for error. We were officially rushing to make our flight on time. There was little room to breathe in the car as Kaitlyn took two clean, fearful boys to the airport. We didn't know it yet, but we would not be coming back the same.

My mom and grandparents were already at the airport, waiting to send us off when we arrived. *Put bag down. Hug Mom. Walk to kiosk.* Still keeping things simple in my mind, I was so happy to have family there. It made the whole process so much easier. I spent thirty minutes with Kaitlyn and my family before my anxiety demanded I go and wait by the gate until takeoff. I got my ticket, and it was time to walk through security. *Oh shit, this is happening.*

Saying goodbye was not easy for me or Kaitlyn. I at least had something daunting in front of me to put all my effort and energy into, keeping my mind distracted. However, Kaitlyn later told me that she could only think about the distance that would soon come between us as she watched me fret about the airport. But we managed to keep our emotions in check, knowing that I would be home soon enough. With a final hug from everyone, it was time to go. *I'll see you all soon.* Weeks later, Kaitlyn and I confessed that tears were shed by both parties as soon as I was out of sight.

I sat in front of the gate in a tense silence. Waiting for our turn to board the plane was like an IV drip of anxiety and excitement. It was our turn to get on the plane. *Oh shit, this really is happening.*

Geoff and I awkwardly walked down the aisle of the plane, trying to avoid anyone's shoulders hitting our side-ass. As we took our seats, the pilot said we might be a little late taking off because of runway traffic. *Oh, great, we might miss our connecting flight.*

Even though my fear of being late was poking at my anxiety, like a curious kid seeing if the snake is alive, I listened to the engines of the plane warming and couldn't help but enjoy the moment. I felt gut-wrenching adrenaline, and an intrigue at the unknown—all the while drowning in a fear that I might fail.

The plane eventually took off, and I looked down to see the East Coast getting farther and farther away. *I'll see you soon.*

Run. That's all I could think as Geoff and I sprinted

at full speed through the Boston airport. The pilot hadn't lied; we were late, really late. I checked my watch in hopes that I had misread the time, but it really was eight o'clock. *Our connecting flight was scheduled to take off two minutes ago! Run faster.* After sprinting past TSA agents and old ladies eating Cinnabons, we showed up to the gate as they were closing the doors.

"Wow. That was a close one, guys," said the lady at the gate, who forcefully smacked her lips together as she spoke. "Hurry on in. The plane is taking off soon."

The city lights faded away as I checked my watch. Total time in Boston: ten minutes. I watched a few minutes of *Swamp People* as the plane reached cruising altitude, still trying to get my heart rate down. The distraction helped keep my anxiety suppressed long enough for the plane to land in Seattle, Washington, where we would finally start pedaling.

As the plane inched toward the ground, my confidence began to soar. I only wished the certainty in myself were matched by the trust I had in the airline managing our luggage. The plane landed. We made our way to the baggage claim, and it was as if my thoughts had predicted the future; we couldn't find the bikes. The box with our trailer and random assortment of gear came right down the carousel, just like everyone else's. But our bikes were missing.

I wasn't going to let anything ruin my attitude. *So*

what? Our bikes aren't here yet. I just need to stay calm, and everything will work itself out. At least that's what I was trying to think. My mind was in chaos with the thought of my bike being lost somewhere in the abyss that lies right behind those gross flaps of thick plastic that every bag emerges from. We waited and waited as my nerves became increasingly unstable. *It's almost midnight. That's it. If I don't go for a walk, I'm about to lose my freaking cool.*

I left Geoff at the carousel so I could burn off some nerves walking across the airport. With my head down, and anxiety up, I struggled to walk calmly and caught myself power walking with sweat starting to bead up. *Take a look around and walk as fast as other people. The guy on the phone is nearly sprinting, so not a good pace. The girl taking a bite of her sandwich is nearly stumbling over the child in front of her, also not a good example to follow. The security guard by the carousel is just standing by those boxes, so that's definitely not a good pace. Wait. Those are bike boxes!*

I went and checked to make sure they were ours, then nearly sprinted back to Geoff to tell him the good news. We were both relieved to have found them, until we noticed that Geoff's box had a massive hole in its side. He frantically stuck his hand in the hole and dug around.

"Dude, I think my seat fell out." When we'd packed the bikes up, we'd had to take the seat posts off so the bikes would fit in the boxes. We'd thought the seats would be fine just lying in the bottom of the box, which they would have, had a giant hole not been ripped open. *Well, shit.*

OK. We need to find a bike shop and buy a new seat post and seat, which are not cheap. Our super tight budget just got a lot tighter, and all of this before we even have our bikes assembled. Damn. What a good way to start the trip....

"Oh, never mind. I found it," Geoff said with a sigh of relief. *My nerves do not need any help freaking out, but thanks for the jump-start, Geoff.*

I donned my book bag, reached down, and began pushing my bike box and the random box toward the door. If it weren't for my friend Ashley, we would be assembling our bikes right there at the airport. She'd generously agreed to let us stay with her for a few days to get set up. Standing in the airport pickup area, I gave her a call to let her know we were there. Two minutes later, she pulled up in a small two-door truck. *Dang, she's fast.*

Her permanent smile was a much needed welcome to Seattle. After hugs and introductions, I opened up the covered truck bed and wondered if everything would fit. She seemed confident that it would; myself, on the other hand, only needed the smallest of reasons to freak out. As we began loading everything in, my blood pressure started to rise from the anxiety of not being able to fit it all, but in the end, the truck bed closed, and we crammed into a single seat in the front. *I'm so glad we don't have to build our bikes in the middle of the night at the airport. Thank God for friends.*

We made it to Ashley's house, pulled into the garage,

and left everything in the truck. The emotional roller coaster of the day had left me exhausted, and I wanted nothing more than to sleep.

As we walked inside, we met Ashley's boyfriend, Dave, whose permanent smile matched Ashley's. After a quick chat about what we were doing and why we were doing it, Dave said, "You can sleep here" (as he pointed to the blow-up mattress), "or here" (as he pointed to a real bed on the other side of the room). I didn't realize it then, but that would be the farthest distance Geoff and I would sleep from each other for a long time… and we were still in the same room. Somehow I got the blow-up mattress, but I didn't care. I fell asleep before my head hit the pillow.

I smell coffee.

My mind instantly exploded with the anticipation and excitement of what the new day would bring, but my eyes stayed glued shut. My adrenal glands were already on high alert, but the rest of my body was struggling to move. *I hear doughnuts.* That unmistakable sound the yeasty treat's box made as someone in the kitchen struggled to get it open made me wake from the dead. *I can't believe there are dough-nuts; this has to be a dream.*

As I stood up, I was welcomed by a cheerful, "Good morning." It was Dave. He looked like he'd been awake for hours. *How long have I been asleep?*

"There are doughnuts and coffee if you want them," Dave said.

Airport

Hell yeah, I thought as I did a happy dance toward them.

"After y'all get ready, we can go to church if you want," he said as he stared curiously at me, most likely because in my effort to contain my giddiness, I looked like a zombie, twitching and solely focused on food.

That afternoon, after church, we drove the truck to Ashley and Dave's storage unit to start building our bikes. About four years earlier, I had worked at a bike shop as a salesman and mechanic. I loved that job and still have a couple of regrets about leaving it. But while I was there, it was no big secret that I belonged on the sales floor and not in the shop. I have a lot of skills, but me in the mechanic's shop was like a milk bucket under a bull's tit.

As we started unpacking the bikes in the storage unit, I had a gut feeling that I would not be able to put this bike together, even though I had managed to take it apart—always biting off more than I could chew. I took the box cutter and began to open the bike box. As I did, the blade caught on something, and being the "act first, think second" type of person I can often be, I tried slicing the box harder. Finally, it cut through, and I managed to unpack the box. I stared at the scattered bike parts on the concrete and wondered if I could get the bike reassembled, the wheels trued, the brakes adjusted, and the gears tuned before nightfall.

It took us a couple of hours, but I eventually put my multi-tool down, thinking we had successfully assembled our bikes. I stood back to admire my work and noticed that I had sliced a section of my shifter cable housing clean off, exposing the cable underneath. *That's what I get for not thinking through things, I guess.* I hopped on the bike to see if everything worked, and luckily it did. Growing up in the South, I had learned that "if it ain't broke, then don't fix it," so I considered this a job well done; well, at least it was done.

That night we partied. Probably harder than someone who was about to do the most labor-intensive work of his life should party, but that's how life goes. When life throws you lemon drops, you drink them. It was a fantastic night spent with amazing people, including some of the most wild, fun-loving, caring people I've ever met.

I was first introduced to Ashely and the rest of the group a few years earlier in Jamaica. I was working there with a humanitarian organization when this group came to the island with a heart to help the locals. We worked on building a schoolhouse, built some outhouses for two families, and painted a church all in one week. Everyone in that group, and the rest of Seattle, showed us a generosity and kindness that could not have set a better tone for the trip.

Ochre Arches And Brick Pillars

My entire life, I have been driven. Well, my friends and family would say stubborn or hardheaded, but I know that it's my tenacious personality that either attracts people to me or pushes them away. It applies to everything that I want to do. "Want" being the key word there, because I can avoid responsibility as well as anyone else. But if I say, "I want that," then I do everything within reason, and otherwise, to get it.

My tour story started years before I landed in Seattle as I walked to the cafeteria during my sophomore year of college and saw a girl. She was walking back to the dorms wearing a red scarf, green jacket, and blue jeans. Her hair was short, and briefly glancing up from the sidewalk, she smiled at me like she could read my mind. I immediately knew that I was going to marry her. I even told Kenny, my roommate, that I was going to meet, date, and marry her.

We spent weeks passing each other, day after day, at the same place on the sidewalk. I asked around and found out her name was Hannah. *Good, at least now I know who I have a crush on.* After about a month of goofy smiles and hellos, I had the guts to ask her if she wanted to walk with me. *I know, I'm a brave, bold soul.* The first words ever spoken in conversation were about the weather. I wish we'd just jumped right into the turmoil we later shared, instead of wading around in such innocent subjects, building up an emotional attachment with our playful banter.

The private, Southern Baptist college we attended did not allow boys and girls to be in the same dorm room at the same time. The most obvious reason for this was to help increase the pent up sexual tension of the school, making the school seem more elite and therefore eligible for higher tuition rates. So, skirting the rules, we hung out in hallways, on the sidewalk, in lounges, and in the back seat of cars. One evening, nearly three weeks after our first walk, we watched a movie in a stairwell on a laptop. Leaning up against the wall with the computer in my lap, we were more than content just being in each other's company. As romantic as the moment was, I couldn't help but start to pay attention to what was happening in my pants. It was getting warmer and warmer by the minute until it felt like I was catching fire. I wish it were more risqué, but it was just the computer overheating and melting my legs off.

After succumbing to the pain, I had to change it up and wanted to do something a bit risky. *Should I ask her to go skydiving or should we just break into the auditorium?* Exploring new places and sneaking around inside of empty buildings was always a good time. However, our first break-in was quite possibly the most permissible break-in the world has ever seen; I mean, the front door was open. But that made it no less entertaining.

She's a daredevil. Nice. Taking note, I knew I needed to make this moment special. She risked a demerit from a mediocre university to break in with me. It was time to get creative.

"Lay down on your back right here like this," I said as I pointed to the middle of the stage.

Oh man… this is either going to be awesome or I am going to be humiliated out of this school and become a salesman at a failing paper supply company.

I laid down on my back, with our feet away from each other and our heads touching so we could both look up at the same thing.

"Look," I said, "there's Orion's belt! Oh, and there's the Big Dipper."

Laughing, she nudged her face against mine and pointed at the lights blinking on the overhead projector.

"Right there?" she said

"Yeah, you see it?! And there is Leo and Scorpius!" I

said enthusiastically, mostly because I couldn't believe this was working.

Hannah told me later she thought that moment was going to be our first kiss. *That's right. I have so much game I keep them waiting. Or, I'm oblivious and have no game at all. The world may know, but I have no idea.*

The day after our "break-in," we went on a walk, and I asked her if she wanted to make our relationship Facebook official, and she said yes. I couldn't believe it! I knew the constellations in the projector would work! I was one step closer to marrying the girl from the sidewalk, and I was ecstatic! I went back to the dorm, chest out and strutting about until Kenny finally asked why I was peacocking around.

"I told you I would marry her," I said. "I told you."

Kenny rolled his eyes and laughed his big deep belly laugh. It was a great day, a better night, and it was all making me very hungry, so I got all the guys together and we went to our nightly eatery, Taco Bell, to celebrate.

It wasn't twenty-four hours after I asked her to be my official girlfriend that I got the bad news. She said that she'd changed her mind, and dating wouldn't be a good idea. I should have known right then that pursuing her was not going to be a healthy option for me, but I was determined. I guess that was the moment when any bit of self-preservation and pride that I had took a lunch break for a while, a long while.

I could stop this chapter right now and repeat the story I just told. The outcomes were the same. The romantic endeavors got better, but the wild ups and downs of our relationship continued.

We rode the proverbial roller coaster for almost three years and it wouldn't be until years after our relationship ended that I resolved the damage caused from the emotional warfare.

Washington

Cheap internet panniers packed, water bottles filled, trailer loaded, spandex on: it was time to start. We'd racked our minds ad nauseam, trying to think of anything that could go wrong, and done our best to prepare for it. There was nothing left to do except start pedaling. I don't know if I was more nervous at the airport or at that exact moment, but either way, my nerves were making me check and recheck everything just to keep busy. *Did I pack the tool kit? Yes. Recheck it. It's still there. Are you sure? No. Check again.* That back and forth in my head would not stop. We probably could have left hours earlier, but we were busy procrastinating and rechecking everything. It was September 3rd at 11 AM, and we could delay no longer. One of my friends that we'd hung out with the night before called her family tree and found us a place to stay in Tacoma, Washington, with Scott. We had to be there that night, which didn't seem hard. It was only forty miles away. No problem.

Ashley and Dave waved us off with some good lucks and farewell pictures. There was nothing left to do except pedal stroke number one. It was incredibly daunting, but we began our journey strong, with no idea what would come next. By pedal stroke ten and not even out of Dave and Ashley's sight, we ran into our first problem, a speed bump.

Ever since I'd purchased the cheap, canvas panniers, I'd wondered if the creators had planned on anyone using them for touring across the country. The bags had two rubber hooks on the back, which were supposed to sit snugly on the top bar of my bike rack. Gravity was supposed to do the rest and keep the bag in place. I guess they didn't expect anyone to hit a pothole or a speed bump because when I gently went over this hump, it seemed like I had just slammed into a concrete fortress. My panniers went flying off my bike, crashing into my spokes, causing me to come to a screeching halt. Luckily I didn't fall, but my pride was incontestably at an all-time low. I'm sure Dave and Ashley had some doubts at that point, too.

Dave ran over and helped me secure my panniers by strapping a bungee cord around them. After we reassembled my gear, I had a bike with a bike rack, two bright red bags strapped onto the sides of the rack with a bungee cord, a pillow and sleep pad on top of the rack, and a sleeping bag tied to my handlebars with some rope. *I am a professional hobo.*

After about ten minutes of riding and a blackberry-picking detour, I hit a sewer drain. Hitting the curb or running over a sewer would typically not be a big deal if I were on a joyride or even training, but that wasn't the case. I was loaded down with at least eighty pounds of gear, and my center of gravity was way off. I gently hit the sewer drain, and bags went flying in the air again. Expecting the same abrupt stop as last time, I braced myself and was able to stop on the side of the road. I got off to put everything together once again, but this was not going to be as easy. The bungee cord had gotten tangled up in my back wheel and now resembled a bird's nest. Not only that, but the bottom corner of my pannier had been ripped to shreds by my spokes, exposing my gear in the bag. *There is no way I can do this across America. No way.*

Now, I'm not sure if it was luck or if Dave had a superpower of being at the right place at the right time, but a moment later, he came driving up behind us as if he were following to make sure I wasn't crashing every ten yards. He handed me a doughnut and set about fixing the bike like he had been doing it his whole life. We added another bungee cord, changed the way we tied the panniers down, and off Geoff and I went… again, again.

I can't crash for a third time today. My pride can't handle it. Luckily, I didn't. It took us almost seven hours, but we made it to Tacoma as the sun set.

Washington

I cannot believe it took us that long to ride only forty miles! I usually get that mileage done in around three hours, not seven! Well, I also don't crash, don't have eighty pounds of gear, don't have to ride up hills that are steeper than a cliffside, and I usually don't get lost every ten minutes either. All in all, a horrific day, to sum it up, but we were three miles away from our first night's sleep, and I was looking forward to it more than eating, which is saying a lot.

We had heard rumors of the "Tacoma aroma," but we had not expected the fierceness of the odor. The aptly given name was spot on with the city's mixture of low tide and paper mill stenches invading my nose like aromatic terrorists. It was precisely the smelling salts I needed to motivate me up South 21st Street.

I'd spoken to our host, Scott, earlier that evening on the phone, and he'd given me oddly specific directions on how to get to his house. Mentally following his route on the map, it seemed like he was telling us to zigzag around his neighborhood. I gave a muted laugh when he explained that there was a hill he was trying to help us avoid on South 21st Street. *I've ridden over plenty of mountains in my time, sir. I'll be fine.*

"Thanks for the heads up," I said, and disregarded his warnings.

No way. "Dude, I'm so tired. This is nuts," I told Geoff as we looked up at South 21st Street, which was so steep we had to crane our necks to do so. The road was only a mile long but went up a hundred meters in a stair-like pattern, which meant that the road was steep as hell, then flat as it crossed an intersection, then so steep I needed a climbing ax to get up it, then flat as a note on American Idol outtakes.

"We have to," Geoff said. "It's the quickest way there, and we're already hours late. I don't want to keep him waiting." Geoff was always the schedule-driven one of the two of us.

And so we started up the first section of the hill, and I put all I had into every pedal stroke. *If Geoff wants to go up this hill, he's going to do it behind me.* Then I coasted to the next section. Rinse and repeat until I felt gassed. I couldn't breathe, much less keep powering up the hill sections. I looked back, and Geoff was off his bike, pushing it up the hill. *Thank God.* I got off my bike and followed suit. It was a defeating moment for both of us, but even more of a severe reality check. Working at camp, I'd had zero time to train for this trip, plus I knew that I was going to be working out for the next few months anyway, while on the trip. *Why should I train to work out?* Because of hills and moments like this one. That's why I should have trained. But there we were, pushing our bikes up a staircase mountain, defeated and tired.

We finally made it to the first night's sleeping spot, elated to have friends with a family kind enough to let us stay. Scott was our very first "road host" and seemed to be the perfect person to introduce us to sleeping in strangers' houses. He had a roommate whose first inclination after meeting us was to pour everyone a much-needed glass of whiskey to help soothe the pain of the night's defeating mountain climb. The warm serum made us euphoric to be done with the day's ride and helped us forget how sore we would be the next day. We shared stories and talked about the overwhelming "Tacoma aroma" until the whiskey told us it was time for bed. We rolled out our sleep pads on the hardwood floor and slept, undisturbed and without a clue what would happen the next day.

I went to sleep excited to fulfill my end of a bargain between Geoff and I, and to pull the trailer the next day. At some point during that first day of riding, it had become glaringly obvious that pulling the trailer was substantially more difficult than carrying the panniers. We had agreed to alternate who pulled the trailer and who used the panniers, switching every other day. After the first day, I would have done anything to not use those damn cheap panniers.

A Mountain Of Pig Meat

I watched for years as Hannah wrestled with her own emotions, as we dated on and off. She needed a guy who would help nurture her relationship with God, but I could not be that person. My parents had been divorced a few years at that point, but I was still mad at the church, and anything else that reminded me of my childhood. I was in full rebellious early-adult mode. Hannah needed someone more stable, but saw my potential to be great. She often said she loved me, telling me how great I was and how my spontaneity kept her on her toes; but I knew she wanted more from me. She was patient for years, waiting for me to grow into the person she knew I could be. I went to Illinois to show her and her parents that I was growing up and drifting away from my rebellious stage. More importantly, I wanted to move the relationship forward.

It was day two of my weeklong trip to Illinois over the summer break. Hannah and I talked about getting married often, but she wasn't fully committed yet. However, in my bull-headed approach to happily-ever-after, I wanted to ask for her parents' approval for when Hannah did finally want to say 'I do.'

The first few days of the trip were extremely busy, visiting with her family, discussing books, going to the batting cages, and attending nightly interrogations from the relatives. But while Hannah was at work on the third day, I eventually had an opportunity alone with her dad, a mustachioed man who resembled Walter Cronkite. It felt like my tongue was made of Jell-O while we were talking, but I managed to say, "Can I marry your daughter?" in the most nervous way possible. After a three-and-a-half hour discussion, he gave me his blessing. I sat back confidently in my chair, feeling like a king, but I was freaking out in my head. *Yes! Yes! I knew I would marry Hannah. I knew it!*

That's all that happened. The story is over. Hannah and I drove off into the sunset, blaring punk rock songs, ready to take over the world. At least, that's what would have happened if fairy tales were real. But life is not an agreeable happy story with a minor conflict in the middle, wrapping up nicely with a comedic punch line or high-level moral guidance. Life continues on, kicking humanity again and again with brief moments of rest and recovery. We just need to catch our breath and keep fighting forward.

The next day I got some alone time with Hannah's mom, who had enough children to start her own show on TLC. I should have kept that in mind when she started asking me about my life goals and what I wanted to do after college. I told her about wanting to ride my bike across America, hike the Appalachian Trail, climb Everest, and run with the bulls, all the while having a job as a physical education teacher. If the conversation had stopped there, my entire life might have turned out differently, but that's not the way life works. One moment changes everything. All the time.

"So, do you want kids?" she asked.

"Oh no, I wouldn't have any time to do the things I want to do. Spending all my time on adventures wouldn't be fair to the kids," I said.

That was it. That sentence, which in all honesty was true at the time, turned this sweet lady into Michael Myers. Our conversation came to an end, and she didn't say much for the rest of the evening. I went to bed that night with a sense of dread, knowing that I had done something wrong, but not quite able to figure out what it was. The day turned into night, and the next morning I awoke to the potent smell of bacon. It was like a hundred pigs had perished in a house fire. It was glorious.

It's a well known fact among my inner circle that I love bacon. I do mean love it. We're talking agape love. It's serious. So, of course, I was pumped waking up to this perfect smell, but when I walked into the living room, Hannah's dad was sitting there reading the paper. Without a smile, he said, "My wife made all of that bacon for you this morning."

"Thank you," I said, confused at his demeanor.

Holy shit. A hundred pigs really did die for this. There was a mound of crispy delicious pig meat stacked nearly a foot tall and even longer wide. I didn't know it at the time, but that was Hannah's mom telling me to get the hell out. *A swine sacrifice to me.*

Hannah and I had a great day spending time at her sister's house and around town. It's hard to remember where we went because any time I think of Illinois, I can only remember the cement roads, the gross amount of liquor stores, and corn. We headed back home after lunch, and before I got into the house, Hannah's dad pulled me aside and asked to speak with me for a second. Alone.

It took three-and-a-half hours to get his blessing and about ten seconds for him to take it away. I guess momma bear had spoken with him at some point, and he was the messenger. Hannah's mom would do anything in her power to make sure her bear cubs kept the circle of life moving forward, which meant that I was no longer to be a part of Hannah's life.

"I don't want you to marry my daughter. You have been a guest here long enough. Please leave," he said.

That was it. I never saw Hannah again.

Of course, I am lying. I did leave Illinois without her parents' blessing, but it was only a matter of days before the cycle of yes, no, rinse, and repeat continued up again. But it was all different now knowing we would never get married because Hannah would never disobey her parents. Our last few months together were plagued with heartache, whether we were alone or together, so we tried to use the cause of our pain as our cure. No amount of consoling one another would have ever helped.

For years up to this point, our off and on relationship had a looming question that stayed near the forefront of our minds: am I the right person? Hannah believed that there was only one person whom God had chosen to be with her. Sometime after my trip to Illinois, she described true love like a bull's-eye, where you can fit multiple darts in the center, but there is only one perfect center. I'm assuming it was her attempt at saying, "You're damn close to perfect, but I want more." She had wrestled with this for years because my beliefs and actions were so close to what she wanted out of her partner, but not quite there. As if somehow I was on a path that paralleled her perfect partner's.

We both knew that the love we shared was real and painfully deep, but like a foreign object underneath the skin, it was being pushed out, picked at, and agitated until it was gone. One big-ass splinter that would leave one big-ass scar.

A Mountain of Pig Meat

There is no way to ever define a relationship with a simple definition. To do so would void all of the little things that made it unique, but it is possible to identify aspects of a relationship. If I were to put an umbrella term on the connection between Hannah and me, I would say it was emotional addiction, a constant need to follow what felt good. If things didn't feel good in the relationship, even momentarily, then we either ran away or ignored it instead of working through the problem. Relationships take work, and we were only willing to chase the easy and temporary dopamine drip. It made sense at the moment, but the long-term effects were devastating.

Six Feet From Us

From Tacoma, Geoff and I rode forty miles to a campground on the outskirts of Olympia called Columbus Park. We decided not to go any further since it was the first time we had to set up our campsite. On the shoreline of a picturesque lake, it took two grown-ass men almost two hours to figure out how to properly set up our tent, sleeping bags, hammock, and clothesline. *We've got to get faster at this.* It took us so long to set up camp that the sun had started to dip below the tree line.

We didn't want to, or rather, we didn't have the discipline to cook rice and beans, so we went up to the camp store to look for some quick eats. That was when we met the camp host, a jolly bearded fellow who could have incontestably passed as Santa. *I had no idea that Santa loved talking about his hot rod so much.* After he gave us a warm welcome to the camp, he showed us around a bit while we chatted. I did learn in the thirty-minute conversation that river rocks are used by some car aficionados to clean the white walls of a classic car tire, another fun fact that I will probably never use, but will always remember.

As we rode through Centralia, Washington, the next afternoon, thirty miles from where we'd started that day, we wanted to stop and sleep for the night. I tried to maintain an optimistic appearance to keep team morale high, but on the inside I was kicking myself for not being able to go further. *I used to ride seventy miles in half of a day, and now I'm struggling to go more than thirty in a full day.* Geoff said it was the panniers' and trailer's weight, but I was too stubborn to pass off my shortcomings on a couple of extra pounds attached to my bike. Nevertheless, I was exhausted and wanted to sleep.

Having thought we found our Mecca nest for the night at a park with the largest pine trees I'd ever seen, we were more than disappointed when it turned out less than perfect. *This place is a shithole.* The "park" was really just a picnic area with moss-covered benches and a shaky roof on the picnic pavilion, accompanied by a hole in the ground to use for relieving oneself. *No thanks.* We decided to try the next campground, a couple of miles down the road.

As we pulled out of the less-than-perfect park, a red-headed cyclist with a fully unzipped jersey, flapping behind him like a cape, came speeding by, giving us the standard head nod. "Standard" in that it was not the chin-up nod that most young people do, but the nose-down nod in an "I acknowledge your presence but do not wish to speak, while respectfully passing by" way. His bike was fully loaded with front and rear panniers, so I knew he was touring pretty far. Geoff and I had not seen anyone else bike touring and our curiosity got the best of us, so we chased the caped redhead.

Nearing a red light a half-mile down the road, I thought we had caught him, but the light turned green, and he got away. By the time we reached the light, it was a solid red again. We gave up the chase, either because it had become a bit creepy at that point or because we were tired, but either way, we stopped to catch our breath.

Geoff and I pulled over to where the asphalt met the grass and took a moment to figure out where we were because, in the heat of the chase, we had become lost. I looked at the map but could not pinpoint our location. I couldn't even begin to orient myself before an ear-piercing screech began rattling my brain. The sound went on forever. *Root canals do not take this long.*

I looked up. A black sedan, heading in our direction and speeding through the red light, got slammed in the passenger side door by a gray Honda Civic that had the green light. Tiny flecks of glass grazed my face. A turn signal cover slid across the asphalt and gently came to rest beside my front tire. *What just happened? No, what is happening?* The

Civic continued careening toward us, spinning. The impact shoved the black car to our right. A reflection of the sun bounced off of the headlight. The black car jumped the curb, missed the transformer box by inches, slammed into the ditch, and came to a stop. Ten feet away, the Civic's rims were now spinning backward. Eight feet away, the car turning clockwise, I could smell the smoke. *Rest. Blink. Breathe.* Seven feet away, the car pointed in the direction it had come from, as if to say, "I want to go back, where it is safe," but it was too late.

The chaos stopped.

Five feet closer and I would have gone home early, in a cast, or worse.

The man in the Civic got out and started throwing his hands in the air and saying things like, "Who drives like that?!" and "The light was clearly fucking red!" *OK. He's fine and doesn't need my help.*

His dog in the backseat had his paws on the window and what looked like a smile on his face. *He's good, too.*

I dropped my bike and ran over to the black car in the ditch. As I opened the driver's door, she looked at me in horror. Bright red was streaming down her face, from what looked to be a laceration on the top of her head. *At least she's conscious. Check the backseat.*

A child, no more than five years old, sat in the middle seat, frozen in fear. His blue eyes contrasted the red liquid on his face, making them vibrant and a focal point for his fearful expression. *He's cut on his head, too?*

I opened the back door to help the child. The woman started screaming. "We're fine! Don't call the police! We don't need help!"

"You're both going to be OK, but y'all are bleeding pretty badly," I said. "The folks across the street at the gas station have already called the police and the ambulance will be here shortly."

"Why!? You shouldn't have done that!" she said. "This is just hair dye that we didn't wash out."

I took another look and noticed the red liquid was just slightly too bright to be blood. I poked my head in again to see if the child was bleeding, and he was fine. *What the hell?*

Aside from poor hair dye jobs, these two seemed fine and didn't need my help. I backed out of the backseat as the firefighters and police showed up. *Wow. That was fast.* Stepping out of the way, I let the professionals do their job and figure out what was really going on.

That was when we met the caped, redheaded cyclist.

After the crash, Jessie—the redheaded cyclist—came cresting over the hill in front of us to see what all of the noise was. He said he was riding from Seattle to St. Augustine, Florida, which made Geoff and I look at each other and smile.

"That's exactly where we're going too," Geoff said, which was close enough to the truth. We planned on ending in Florida, but didn't have an exact city to end in. "Where are you staying tonight?"

After a quick conversation about the chaos of the wreck, we decided to group up and head to the next camp-site. We rode together for weeks.

Learning Curve

The ride the next morning, from Columbus Park to the Lewis and Clark Campground, was forty-four miles of absolutely stunning country. The winding, hilly roads took Jessie, Geoff, and I through the crisp, foggy weather and showed us all the beautiful pine trees and ferns that Washington had to offer.

At the Lewis and Clark State Park, I woke up intensely cold, like arctic weather cold. *I can't feel my ass.* I peaked my head out from my sleeping bag, and all I could feel was cold water soaking through the tarp onto my arm. *No wonder, it's thirty-five degrees, and I'm soaking wet. I feel like a snowman pissed on me.* The overhead tarp would have worked, but it was pressed up directly against my hammock, allowing the dew to soak straight through. My sleeping bag absorbed most of it, making what should have been my comfy cocoon into a heavy hypothermic hell hole. My ass never stood a chance at being warm.

I learned a lot that night. First, I learned to always use a sleeping pad, even in the hammock. It's a rule I learned years ago, but in a drunken stupor I had decided to tough it out. *Note to self: don't make stupid mistakes after drinking.* The second lesson learned that night was to make sure the tarp had enough excess to wrap around my cocoon, without touching me, avoiding the dew altogether. Lastly, and most importantly, the next morning I learned to always carry enough quarters to the bathroom when showering on the West Coast. Unfortunately, I only had enough change to get two minutes of lukewarm water. *Get the pits, stick, and quit.*

Even a short shower was very much needed since we had worn the same clothes for two days and not showered. I didn't have enough time to get all the stink off of me, but at least I went from smelling like a dead skunk to a live skunk. As I slid into my cold, damp clothes from the day before, I started laughing. I couldn't believe that this was going to be the norm for the next... however long. *I'm tired, my legs are killing me, my butt feels like it's been through a meat grinder, and I can't believe it's already this cold in September!* There was nothing else to do except laugh and try to get comfortable being uncomfortable.

After we made the pathetic attempt at drying everything out in the Pacific Northwestern fog, we packed up camp and rolled out. Leaving the campground and starting the day's ride, I was pumped for the adventure but wasn't sure my legs could handle another day of abuse. I was a weekend warrior putting my legs through a proper training regimen with no days off and terrible sleep. It would take a solid ten miles before I warmed up enough to get moving competently, but it took Jessie about ten seconds before he took off ahead of us. We tried to keep up with him for about a mile, but it wasn't happening. We were loaded down too heavy, and the trailer created too much drag. Luckily, we knew we were headed in the same direction.

We caught up to Jessie north of Astoria, Oregon, along the north side of the Columbia River. As Geoff, Jessie, and I rode along the winding river, I couldn't stop day-dreaming about fishing. It was an almost primal instinct taking over my senses. I watched the water as it passed around islands and over rocks, thinking about where the fish could be. Maybe I really would have caught a record-breaking trophy, had we stopped to fish, or perhaps the day-dreaming was just me wanting to take my mind somewhere else for a moment. Either way, we pedaled on.

We rode forty-five miles to a campground called County Line Park, where we made camp right along the river. I wanted to go fishing so much it hurt, but moving my legs also hurt, so I listened to my body and relaxed in the hammock. As I lay with my legs stretched out over the hammock's side, the camp host came up and introduced herself. She was an intensely heartwarming woman, with a smile that would not go away. After chatting for about an hour, she decided to let us stay there for free, which kept the trend of West Coast generosity alive.

The Pacific Northwest emphatically stole my heart with its scenic hills and fantastic fishing city/village persona. We were just days into the trip, and I already loved every city and quaint town I'd had the privilege of going through. The locals were incredibly kind, always sharing their food or letting us stay for free. My heart was changing for America, and I looked forward to where it ended up.

The three of us woke up the next morning and planned on making it forty miles to Astoria. We knew Astoria was where they had filmed *The Goonies*, and like any nostalgic tourists, were looking forward to seeing the Goonies House. Everything else Astoria had to offer would be a surprising bonus. At some point along the way, as we crossed over a bridge, we decided to pull over for a quick bite to eat. The bridge ended at a large shoulder off the side of the road. As we pulled onto it, we noticed a trail heading down to the river. Naturally, being the curious-minded one, I hopped off my bike and jogged down the path, jumping off a small cliff near the bottom onto river rocks. I yelled out to Geoff and Jessie, "You've got to see this!"

Geoff dragged both of our bikes down the trail, and I carefully lowered them down the small cliff. It was work, but it was worth it. Tied to the underside of the bridge was a rope swing dangling above the crystal clear water. Never passing up an opportunity for adventure, we stashed the bikes against the graffiti-laden bridge piling and stripped down to near nakedness. I checked the water depth and noticed two spots in the water with large rocks. *Do not land on those.* I grabbed the rope, walked away from the water, and climbed to the top of a large boulder. With one deep breath, I launched myself over the river and landed in the icy cold water. It was intensely bitter, but the sun was out, and after climbing out and lying on the hot rocks for just a second, I was ready to do it again. This time I had Geoff video call Kaitlyn and did a backflip as the rope reached its highest point. *I love a good stunt, especially if I can impress Kaitlyn.* It was the perfect pit stop.

Looking over the map before leaving, we noticed we had to take a ferry to Astoria, on the south side of the river, which isn't a big deal for most people, but this was my first ever ferry ride, and I was geeking out over it. Or the excitement could have been from eating lunch, which always put me in a better mood. Jessie had had the ingenious idea of putting the gigantic wild blackberries we had gathered along the way onto a peanut butter sandwich. The blackberries were bigger than my thumb and juicier than any fruit I'd ever had. Add a Mountain Dew to the mix, and I was all kinds of jacked up for that ferry ride.

As we approached Astoria, the city seemingly popped

up from behind the pine trees and opened into the most picturesque fishing town I had ever seen. The coastal town was the first semi-big city we rode through, making it the perfect place to get a room and some actual decent sleep. Around two hundred miles and nearly five thousand feet of uphill climbing from where we had first started, my out-of-shape butt needed a break, and Astoria couldn't have been a better spot for it. We unloaded our gear in the closet of some sketchy hostel and rode straight back the way we'd come, to the Goonies House, having ridden right past it earlier. We arrived at the iconic house with another group of tourists, and while the house looked dramatically different from in the movie, I could vividly replay the scenes in my head. It sent me spiraling down nostalgia lane, and I loved it. *This looks like the perfect spot to get some dirt.*

It has always been a challenge to determine my favorite movie. Do I judge it by rewatch-ability, quality of production, the way it makes me feel, plot lines, or acting? There are so many genres and sub-genres that it makes determining a true favorite nearly impossible. Regardless, *Saving Private Ryan* is unquestionably near the top of my list in all regards. For me, the scene where Sergeant Mike Horvath (played by Tom Sizemore) is collecting dirt, and placing it in a tin can marked "France," seemed fitting for my trip across America. In every state we went through, I wanted to collect a small tin of dirt to carry with me. It seemed appropriate for my collection to include the Goonies House, since Hollywood had inspired me to collect dirt in the first place.

We went back to the sketchy hostel after visiting the Goonies House and eating dinner, for some much-needed R and R, which for me meant TV time, of course. Jessie went back out to explore more of the city, and Geoff wrote in his journal. It was a relaxing and rejuvenating night.

The next morning we went to breakfast at a Columbian café where I had the best bacon, hash, and egg breakfast of my life. We sat outside in the crisp weather since we wanted to keep an eye on our bikes. While I was busy shoveling the food in my face, I briefly looked up into the window of the café and saw the barista, a 6' 2" gentleman, wearing a pink cut-off T-shirt that said, "Dance it out Bitch." I erupted in laughter and did absolutely nothing to try to contain it. I loved that saying, and maybe it was the full night's sleep getting to me a little bit, but I felt like I needed that shirt. Luckily, Geoff and Jessie found it just as funny as I did. We kept repeating that saying randomly for weeks. Sometimes screaming it at the top of our lungs, barreling down a mountain, but other times whispering it softly just before bed. It never failed to lighten the mood. *Good job, barista.*

After we wrapped up our meal, we noticed a bike shop nearby. Already carrying more supplies than we needed, we happily went into the shop for more. That was when we met Mike: a six-foot-tall, extremely tan man with grey and black hair that he kept in a bandana. I could tell at first glance that this guy had been on the road for a long time. We quickly started up a conversation, and learned that Mike had been cycle touring for over a year. He was at the shop to get a new tube. What I found odd was that instead of changing the tube himself, he just gave the mechanic his tire to fix. *Why doesn't he do it himself? It's cheaper, and he should have the tools.* On second glance, I noticed he wasn't carrying any tools. He didn't have any saddlebags. He wasn't pulling a trailer, either. He only had a tiny, cylindrical bag that sat on his rear bike rack. "Where's all of your stuff?" I asked naively, knowing he had been on the road for a while.

"I just pay for things as I need them," he said. "I don't carry anything with me, and I eat out at restaurants twice a day." *A credit-card cycle tourist. Well, that's one way to do it.* Mike rode with Jessie, Geoff, and me for a large portion of the day: a bike gang, taking on Astoria.

Unwelcome Guests

It's finally happening. I am starting to feel comfortable. As the miles tallied up along the Oregon coast, we became more open to the adventures and spontaneity of the road and, with it, an understanding that weird things happen. Daily ventures and mishaps were becoming normal; I just never expected normal to be so damn creepy.

Without fail, I managed to stay underdressed for Oregon's mid-September damp chill that never left my skin. The northwestern fog with only occasional sunlight made riding feel like I was always engulfed in the first blast of air from opening a freezer. Geoff was tired of my constant commentating on the cold, the wet, and the suck that we were going through, but he's a patient guy, and it would take weeks before he snapped.

I always voiced my opinion about the cold, the status of my hunger, and when it was time to sleep. I had no timeline or goals for each day's ride, so I would go as fast or as long as Geoff wanted to unless I was hungry or sleepy. I am an extremely irate individual with a short fuse when I am hungry, but give me a bite to eat, and I'm Mary fucking Poppins. On the other hand, when I'm tired, I am like a dying battery with a blinking red light. I have a few moments left, but when I'm out of power, I acutely resemble a sluggish sack of meat.

A few hours past midday, we were riding through a long stretch of rolling hills and thick trees when I gave Geoff and Jessie a pleasant warning that I was getting tired and about ready to fall asleep. Geoff responded like he had every night, with, "OK. Let's keep riding and see if we can find a campsite," which never made any sense because we could be headed into the desert with nothing in sight for two hundred miles, and he would still say the same thing, but that story comes later. Right then, we could have just used the phone and looked for a campsite, but I bit my tongue and kept riding. A few miles later, as if by Geoff magic, we found an RV park and coasted in to check the prices.

All three of us looked around at the empty, overgrown tent sites next to the rundown RVs as we rolled by. I particularly noted the rust running down the sides of multiple campers. *How long have these things been here?* It was unnerving, but weirdness was becoming routine, so I shrugged it off and continued riding toward the main office.

As I was reaching for the front door of the office, Jessie said, "The prices are right here," as he pointed to the price list tacked to a sheet of rotting plywood held up by warped 2 by 4's. *Forty-five dollars!? This is a fucktastic display of bike-path robbery!* The five-dollar hiker/biker sites that littered the West Coast had spoiled us. We couldn't believe that it cost so much to pitch a tent and sleep on the cold, wet ground.

We looked up other places to sleep using Geoff's iPhone, and after seeing that the next campground was a solid twenty miles away, decided to stealth camp for the first time. We had hardly seen any cars drive by as we stood there, and there were even fewer buildings around. After spending the night before in actual beds at the hostel, stealth camping seemed a good way to return to our cycle-touring standards of roughing it. It was our best bet.

Across the main street, a road, overgrown with pine trees, curved as it went up a steep hill. It appeared desolate, dark, and a perfect place to sleep. Comfortably uncomfortable. It took a bit to convince Geoff, but since Jessie was all about it and Geoff didn't want to spend money, we agreed to ride up the ominous hill.

The second we began pedaling underneath the encroaching trees, the sunlight all but vanished. The cozy woodland tunnel would have been amazing if it weren't so terrifying. As we rode up the hill, I kept my eyes at the tree line along the road, looking for a deer path or some entrance into the insanely thick underbrush. At the top of the mile-long hill, the tree line finally broke at a large opening. We neared and saw a fence with a cross on it. *No way, man, this is jacked up. I'm not sleeping here.* The thoughts were screaming in my mind, even as I dismounted my bike, took my helmet off, and scanned the area for anyone watching. I was actively pursuing the exact opposite of what I wanted, but the chest-rattling heartbeats and rapid breathing were only encouraging me to keep going. Besides, the trip was becoming weirder by the day, so it only seemed fitting for us to start sleeping in graveyards.

We discussed the possibility of being caught by security guards or the police, but realized that the gate didn't look very used and the grass was hardly maintained, so our chances of being caught by security or maintenance personnel were relatively low. *But guys, what about the grave robbers and murderers?*

I opened the squeaky gate, noting the cold, wet steel in my hand. We walked our bikes through the gate and paused. I scanned the surprisingly large graveyard, looking for a hill or headstone to hide behind, but there was nowhere to hide all three of us. The thicket of trees on the outskirts of the field looked like it had a small clearing inside, so we walked along the perimeter of the rusted fence line, looking for an opening into the woods. Conveniently, there was a path where the fence met the tree line, which seemed suspicious, but creepy or not, it was the only place we could find cover to make camp. Our bikes were just a bit wider than the path, so moving through the woods was not easy. We were making so much noise, crushing leaves and breaking branches, that I'm surprised we didn't wake the permanent residents of the graveyard.

Finally, we found an opening in the forest, underneath the pine trees where the lower limbs seemed to have been snapped off at the base, creating a perfect circle of protection where we could make camp. We could see the tombstones through the trees in the failing light, but we thought that as long as we didn't pitch the tents, we shouldn't be spotted. So we rolled out the tarp and put our sleeping bags on top. We laid down and folded the excess tarp on top of us, creating a Geoff and Shaun taco tarp in a graveyard. Jessie did the same thing, just feet away from us. *This is normal.*

I tossed and turned, never really getting comfortable enough to fall into a deep sleep. In my half-awake daze, I noted the distant echoes of people talking, but shrugged it off and tried to go back to sleep. Light flashed through my closed eyelids. My eyes slammed open as my adrenaline spiked. I looked out into the graveyard. Four or five people walked around, talking and flickering the flashlights toward the woods where we lay. *Well, busted.* They came closer, and none of us moved. I could sense that Geoff and Jessie were both awake and lying still. The graveyard group came a bit too close for comfort but eventually walked away, allowing me to continue my restless night's sleep.

I woke up with a tree branch so close to my face that I could smell the dew-soaked pine sap. I whispered Geoff's name, and within seconds all three of us were up, packing our sleeping bags away, and rolling our bikes out of the woods. We'd received no warm welcome from our hosts and were given no courteous goodbyes as we left.

It was time to keep heading south, and toward an unwelcoming day. As we stood by the front gate of the graveyard to check the map, I realized I was wet from head to toe: unwelcome guest number one. The water had come on softly, not quite a rain but just damp air. It was a different kind of wet, chilling and unsettling. The water seemed suspended in the air as if I were running into it. We mounted our bikes and headed back through the wooded tunnel.

Exiting the dark woods and onto the main road, back on our original course, we passed the grossly overpriced campground and smiled. We'd won. We hadn't paid to sleep. We'd stuck it to the man, but I wanted unquestionable dominance, so I used their restroom. *Never overcharge again!* I rode away, confident and with an empty bladder.

About ten miles down the road, unwelcome guest number two, and my second biggest fear, erased all my confidence.

Cruising down a series of switchbacks with a smile cannot last forever. Eventually, you have to start pedaling uphill. As a glorious downhill came to an end, and we reached the valley to begin yet another climb, two dogs barreled toward us through a small gap between their owner and a fence post. It must be true that dogs can smell fear because out of all three of us, they came straight for me. I slammed on the brakes, then released them and pedaled harder. *Stop... no, go!* I was having a complete mental shutdown. My mind raced as I envisioned scenes of Jack London's *Call of the Wild* with ravenous dogs ripping me to shreds, leaving my entrails scattered in the middle of the road as Geoff and Jessie watched in horror.

In reality, the dogs showed some gnarly teeth, growled a bit, and left me alone once their owner called them back. *Thanks for not destroying me, dogs. Now, if you wouldn't mind mailing my pride back to me when you finish toying with it, that'd be great. Thanks.*

To add to my broken pride, my knee injury from camp was reminding me that I needed to rest. Every downward pedal stroke made the outside of my knee feel like it was on fire—unwelcome guest number three. At least I could keep moving forward. I rarely listen to my body's needs as long as it's doing what I need it to. *That could explain a lot of daily aches and pains, but who really knows.* Eventually I had to stop for a moment to wrap my knee with an Ace bandage to give it some support. *Just keep moving. I will be fine.*

It had been an unwelcome day for sure, but on top of

it all, Geoff wasn't feeling well. We decided to ride into Bay City, Oregon, and take the next day off. *Wooo hooo!* I needed the rest for my fatigued legs and my immensely sore backside. For graphic details, google "saddle sores." I think the term itself says enough. Dealing with the sores was rough, but the day off was fantastic. We stayed at a city park, which would have been fine, but with a busted-up basketball court, a run-down skatepark, and a camp host who disappeared after the first night, it became a bit sketchy. However, sketchy was becoming our standard.

There was a strong desire to keep riding, but also to rest more, at the same time. I knew I needed the recovery, but I never wanted to be forced to stop for saddle sores. I asked Geoff to let me use his Chamois Butt'r. The application procedure was not something I was used to at the butt crack of dawn, nor did I particularly enjoy a cold, wet cream creating a slip and slide in my pants, but it was completely worth it. It allowed me to spend longer days in the saddle without having severe pain. As a novice triathlete, I had never used Chamois Butt'r and hardly used cycling shorts. But spending long hours in the saddle convinced me that the cons of a momentarily weird feeling before a ride greatly outweigh the discomfort and pain of saddle sores that can last weeks.

The day off was composed of a lengthy itinerary, none of which we completed, and it was fantastic. I laid in the sun, trying my best to unthaw from the damp, cold northwestern weather. I mailed home ten pounds of gear I had not used and deemed unnecessary. Perhaps the best activity of the day, which I did plenty of, was eating. I ate until it hurt, and then I ate a few bites more. To add to this feeding frenzy, we left camp searching for something a bit more appetizing than rice and lentils.

We ended up riding past the Tillamook Beef Jerky Factory Outlet billboard, which read, "Home of the 2 ft pepperoni stick for $1." We arrived at the outlet just in time to catch them closing up shop. Luckily they hadn't locked the doors yet and allowed us to come inside. We gathered a handful of meaty delights that we thought would be good with rice and went to check out. At the register, the cashier asked us if we wanted to take home the samples for the day since they threw out all the leftovers at closing time, anyway. *Holy mother of meat stick heaven. Are you kidding me?! I've died and gone to a land of sodium-packed, processed-to-death, preservative-rich, meat heaven.* We left that factory with between twenty and twenty-five pounds of beef jerky. The unwelcoming day yesterday had turned around.

From the beginning of the trip all the way to Bay City, Oregon, we'd followed a set of maps we'd bought from the American Cycling Association that showed everything from bike shops to places to camp, eat, and sightsee. It was useful to a point, but Geoff and I had become too focused on riding a certain distance, or meeting a specific goal every day, ultimately taking away from the adventure of it all. We decided to use the maps as a guide and not let our goal-oriented nature take over. We would ride until we wanted to stop, and then we would find a place to stay for the night. I was all for the plan, knowing it would force some impromptu, possibly precarious adventures. Jessie would continue to follow his gut instinct and let his journey unfold naturally, whether that meant staying with us or not, as he'd been doing from the beginning.

We woke up in a meat-sweat daze the morning after the beef jerky incident. Jessie had already left for the day. We quickly packed our gear and started pedaling down the West Coast, without any idea where we would end up. As we passed by the beef jerky factory, I stood up on my pedals, gripped the seat between my legs, let go of the handlebars to stand as tall as possible, and gave a salute just as one last thank you.

About twenty miles later, in Sandlake, we stopped to eat. As we pulled off to the side of the road, Geoff hit a surprisingly deep sand patch that brought him to an immediate halt. Even with his years of cycling experience, he stopped so fast that he couldn't get his feet unclipped from the pedals, and he embarrassingly toppled over. It was more of a shameful fall than a crash, but there we were, roughly three hundred miles into the trip and Geoff had his first "crash." I laughed so hard that I cried. I even choked on the peanut butter and jelly tortillas a half hour later, remembering his fall.

We made it only another ten miles before we decided to stop in Pacific City. As we rolled into the campground, we immediately spotted Jessie's tent already set up, but he wasn't around. *It's so weird that we keep staying at the same places. I guess the hills and weather exhaust everyone at about the same rate, and we just want to stop at the same time.* We pitched our tent near his, and he showed up a few minutes later, freshly showered. Minutes later, an SUV pulled into the campsite next to ours, and two women got out. They were surgical in their movements, setting up their elementary campsite quickly. An absurdly large tent, picnic table paraphernalia, and some firewood were all they set up. *The bigger the tent, the more air my body has to heat to keep warm. No way would I camp with that.* As the sun went down, they came over to introduce themselves and asked if we wanted to have a fire on the beach. Since I was the only unavailable guy there, my minority vote wouldn't have mattered. We went to the beach after Montana and April.

By the time Geoff, Jessie, and I showed up, the women had already built a fire and set up a little blanket pad. We were not as prepared and sat on the freezing sand. *At least we have the fire to keep us warm.* As I watched nature's television slowly burn away, I offered to help chop some firewood to keep it going, but Montana, in her Canadian accent, said, "I got it." With one swing of her hatchet, she split the log straight down the middle, making it look as effortless as slicing cheese. *Glad I didn't try. I would have been put to shame just now.*

She picked up the burning logs with her bare hands to place the fresh logs in the perfect spot. *Sorcery.* Never had I seen anyone pick up lit firewood like that. She didn't pick up the part of the wood that hadn't caught fire yet, either; she picked up the shit-hot side and didn't even flinch. Geoff, Jessie, and I didn't say a word, but all looked on in awe. I knew Montana and April could feel us staring because April said, "Yeah, we have to keep fires going most of the year, or else we freeze to death in Canada. Even as children, we were working with fire." *Makes sense. It doesn't mean I'm not impressed.*

A couple of minutes later, April asked if we wanted to hear a song. Praying that agreeing wasn't a mistake, I nodded my head along with Geoff and Jessie. April got out a ukulele, and Montana prepared her harmonica. It was the first time I had ever heard "Wagon Wheel" by Bob Dylan and Ketch Secor, but most famously covered by Darius Rucker. I had not heard music in weeks, but as I sat in the full moonlight on the beach, they played the first chord, and I immediately experienced frisson. The moment entranced us all. They were incredible musicians, and the scene was set for them to deliver a moving performance, but when they sang the line about getting a move on before sunrise because I know that she's the one, I nearly left the beach right then and started riding. I wanted Kaitlyn to be there with me so badly. I wanted her to be experiencing everything that I was.

I was missing our late night pillow talks and the endless inside jokes. I wanted to look across the campfire and see her. I needed to tell her how much I loved her when I got home. When I got home. *Home. I need to go home.*

We woke up the next morning, and Jessie was gone. No note, no goodbye, just gone. He disappeared often, and we always seemed to catch up to him somehow, but this time felt different—more abrupt. Montana and April were not at their campsite, so we could not say goodbye to them either. We left Pacific City as we had come in, a pair of vagabonds, alone together.

Moving On

I have taken comfort in the idea of destiny for most of my life, but it was while riding down the Oregon coast that I realized comfort was something that I couldn't afford anymore. I needed to do something to take back control of my life, which in hindsight is why I decided to ride a bicycle across America. I rode to be uncomfortable. I rode to forget. I rode to grow.

I had a lot of time to think about life while I was riding down Highway 101. The picturesque views helped to frame my thought process as I contemplated my current and previous relationships. As I flipped through my mental Rolodex of memories, I thought about my relationship with Hannah and realized that I had been in love with someone who didn't love me back for years. It took a specific state of psychosis mixed with my resolute mindset to create the framework for our relationship, but it happened. I was desperately in love with a woman who had thrown in the towel long before I had finished fighting. The truth was as clear as I had ever seen it.

I grew up on movies like *The Notebook*. I always emulated the iconic love stories with me being the foolhardy, love-drunk gentleman patiently waiting for and pursuing his love at first sight. The truth was staring back at me so brightly I had to squint. *I swear it's not the sun reflecting off the cars passing by.* I was not going to get my Hollywood love story with Hannah. She was gone. I needed to let her go for good. I needed to be the man I wanted to be, true to myself and my word. I had a woman back home whom I truly loved. I was dwelling in the past.

Self-development is not always pretty and certainly seldom accidental. It took me time and effort to finally start getting over Hannah, but I was on the scenic lookout of Heceta Head Lighthouse in Oregon when I made a conscious decision to never look back at that time in my life with desire in my heart. As I looked over the cliff at the Pacific Ocean, I told myself, this is where I would stop carrying her. *This is the best place I can think of to leave you. From here on, I am riding toward a new relationship, and I can't have you with me anymore; it's not fair to her or me. I hope you found what you were looking for in life. Goodbye.*

It was a day of cleansing for me and one that I wish

would have come much sooner. The rest of the day, I stayed farther back from Geoff than usual as I contemplated everything. It was a weight lifted off of my shoulders, and I felt free.

We rode another sixteen miles to the Jessie M. Honeyman Memorial State Park and finished off the fifty-one-mile day with a delicious bowl of spaghetti. Well, I ate spaghetti. Geoff made a bowl of spaghetti and dropped it on the ground. Furious at his mistake, but knowing he needed to eat, he relit the stove and made another bowl, but managed to spill this one all over himself. He was livid, but we both broke into laughter at his expense. Geoff ate peanut butter and jelly that night.

It must have been enough food because the next day, we rode fifty-four miles and climbed nearly 1,500 feet, which wasn't too bad since almost all of the elevation came in the form of two large hills. We stayed at a campground in Coos Bay, the childhood home of Steve Prefontaine, or "Pre" as he was known. Pre was arguably the best distance runner of all time. A brash and charismatic personality set him apart from all of the other elite runners of the late sixties and early seventies. He was famous for his attitude and record-breaking runs, a perfect role model for Geoff and me. Being in Coos Bay, I took solace in knowing I was riding the same streets that he used to run.

We ended up staying at a campground called "Sunset Bay State Park," where we met Rhea, a short, spunky woman who genuinely loved the outdoors. Rhea was also on a cycle tour along the West Coast, and even at first sight, it was easy to tell she knew what she was doing. The three of us rolled into the park around the same time, looking for where the tent campers were supposed to stay. We found a green patch of grass with a few picnic tables and pitched our tents. Well, Geoff and I pitched our tent. Rhea rolled out her mat underneath the picnic table and as a "just in case" measure, she threw a tarp over the table to act as a rain fly. She was all set up in seconds, while Geoff and I were still unpacking the tent. *This woman is an efficiency genius. We waste so much time setting up and tearing down camp. We've got to get faster.*

Just as we threw our bags into the tent, Rhea came over and offered us some sweet tea, one of the many things from home that I was craving. *Oh, you delicious ode to the South. Get in my mouth.* The hot, sugary, leaf water was perfect. A comfort from home that had the added benefit of taking away the wet, chilly bite of the northwestern fog. I thanked Rhea for the drink and sat down on a nearby stump to enjoy the moment.

I realized I was learning to enjoy the little things. Small details that made up the bigger picture of our lives had become focal points, since every day was nearly the same:

Wake up.

Eat.

Pack up camp.

Eat.

Ride.

Eat.

Set up camp.

Eat.

Sleep.

The days were merging, but the little things were standing out in a big way. *Pay attention to everything, Shaun. You will only be here once.*

"Cooooooo! Goooood morrrrning, everyone!"

The voice was loud and starkly contrasted the peaceful quietness of the morning. I poked my head out of the tent, rubbing the thick, wet gunk out of my eyes to see a balding older man with a long beard chasing after a slow-moving car through the campground. "Cooooo!" he yelled while running after the car. *What the... Why is he... Am I...?* I could not formulate the simplest of thoughts to comprehend why this man was cooing and chasing cars. I awkwardly laughed to shake off the moment, but Geoff couldn't shake it. He brought up "the quail guy" in conversation all day. I couldn't blame him. It was a weird wake-up call, to say the least.

There was no going back to sleep after that, so I got up and put some water in the Jetboil stove to make oatmeal. Eager to start riding for the day, I left the water to boil while Geoff and I packed our sleeping bags and tent. While we were packing, I looked over at Rhea and saw something I never thought I would see.

Rhea had an open packet of oatmeal pinned between her feet. She was standing up with a steaming pot of water in her hands. *No way, she won't do it.* Rhea slowly began to pour the scalding hot water out of her pot and into the oatmeal pouch pinned between her feet. *What?!*

She filled the entire pouch without spilling a drop.

Our time with "the quail man" and Rhea had come to an end, so we finished up our oatmeal, packed away our dishes, and said goodbye as we pedaled off. Quail Man and Rhea taught me a lesson I will never forget: be myself. Those two were true to themselves and displayed a real passion for their lives. They moved effortlessly and with zeal. I learned a lot in just the few moments I spent with them at that campsite, but now we were gone and it was time to ride.

We had climbed nearly a thousand feet in an hour when I noticed a little fish-and-chips restaurant and decided that if I didn't have food right then, I would possibly die. As was our routine, we ate outside to keep an eye on our bikes. The weather had warmed up quite a bit, and the sun was shining, so eating at the rickety, wooden, sun-bleached tables was preferable anyway.

It didn't take long before an aging couple came over and struck up a conversation about our trip. The lady, whose name I never got, offered to let us stay at their mansion and mentioned something about a private jet, all the while thumbing at her pearl necklace. While she described her luxurious lifestyle, she continued to eat popcorn shrimp and talk with her mouth full. Flakes of breaded crustacean dribbled out of her mouth while she spoke. I honed in on the bit of saliva dripping out the corner of her mouth. *Should I tell her? Does Geoff see this? What is she talking about again?* It took every bit of self-control I had to not audibly gag.

We kept riding, choosing not to take a rest day at the mansion. I wasn't sure I could have slept in that house without dreaming of mashed up shrimp bits falling from the ceiling.

The rest of the day was relatively easy, climbing just five-hundred feet over thirty-five more miles, totaling around 1,600 feet of elevation gain in about fifty miles. Having accomplished a fair amount of distance by 5 PM, we decided to stop at the next campground. While cruising down Highway 101, I saw a sign that read "Cape Blanco Campground - 3 Miles" with an arrow pointing down a side road. *Well, that's only a total of six miles out of the way. That's not too bad.*

"Geoff, you want to stay there?" I yelled out, trying to project my voice over the traffic.

"Sure," Geoff said. I could tell the thought of covering extra mileage to sleep wasn't exciting to him. I wasn't over the moon about it either, but we both grudgingly turned right off Highway 101 and onto Cape Blanco Road, not knowing whether the campground was run down or if it would be the highlight of the trip.

We had knocked all the hills out early in the day, the sun was shining, and it was reasonably warm, but almost immediately after turning onto Cape Blanco Road, the weather changed drastically. First, clouds moved in fast. Weirdly fast. *Great, here comes the rain.* But the rain held off for a bit. Then, as if in a horror movie, we rode into a cloud of fog so thick it was hard to see where we were going. The mist brought on the heat-sucking dampness that kept me chilled to the bone. Before we made it to the campground, the sun had all but disappeared, blotted out by the cloud and fog cover.

Just before the last bit of light left for the day, we emerged from a group of trees onto a hill and saw the campground below us through a break in the fog, a surreal view that was so haunting, I never want to see it again. The fog's creepiness combined with a chilling wind and a lighthouse overlooking everything made me uneasy, but we needed a place to sleep. *Quit being dramatic and ride.*

We were greeted with smiles and free firewood as we checked in to the campground. *OK, it's not that bad here. Unless they are serial killers trying to lure us in. The chances of being killed by a serial killer are low, but never zero percent .*

The skies were clear, the temperature was perfect, and I felt great, but I still had chills running down my spine when I thought about the night before. Not to mention, the three-mile backtrack ahead of us was less than ideal. We wanted to get out of there and moving in the right direction quickly, so we decided to forgo breakfast. I hated riding somewhere I'd already been, but I'm sure it was a lack of food that made the quick three-mile trip the worst moment of my life. *Character flaw number 127: When dealing with any minor inconvenience on an empty stomach, I instantly amplify it to "end of the world" status.*

Once we were back on the main road, it didn't take long before my hunger pains demanded I stop and eat immediately. We pulled over on Highway 101. An embankment of rocks was piled high on the outside of the curve to keep people from driving off the cliff and into the water. Geoff and I carried our bikes up and over the rocks. When we finished climbing down the backside of the embankment, we leaned the bikes up behind a huge boulder. I walked along a ledge paralleling the ocean, periodically peeking over the edge of the cliff down to the water a few yards down. I turned a corner and nearly fell off the cliff when I found Jessie hiding out behind a different rock, eating lunch.

"What!? No way!" I said. "Good to see you again, man!" His startled look turned to happy surprise.

We ate lunch together perched on rocks overlooking the ocean. As I put my dishes back into the trailer, Jessie and Geoff climbed the huge boulders that jutted out into the ocean. I went after them, but I should have changed shoes. Wearing cycling shoes on slippery rocks was not the best idea. The cleats that attach to the pedal of the bicycle jut out from the bottom of the sole, which made walking on rocks feel like I was slipping after every step I took. After taking our time, we summited the stones victoriously, staking claim to the rocks if only for a brief moment.

Now, I know that I can't be the only person who gets to the top of a summit and feels a primal urge to throw something off. Indulging my impulses, I threw a torso-sized rock off the boulder and into the water. Geoff and Jessie followed suit. The next rock I threw, I intentionally missed the water so I could see the rock smash below us. To my delight, it exploded when it crashed onto the rocks below, sending shrapnel-like debris everywhere. Three grown men spent the better part of an hour smashing rocks on that boulder. The change of pace was a much-needed break, but it was time to keep riding. We were two days from California and didn't want to get distracted.

We'd made it a few miles down the road when we saw Bigfoot. We can't prove it because his arms and shoulders looked much like those of a human, but Bigfoot was surely driving down the road in an old silver Honda Civic with his fur-covered head hanging out the window. That much I know for sure.

We stealth camped that night somewhere around Wedderburn, which made for a short thirty-five-mile day. *We spent more time smashing rocks than I thought.* But I was happy with what we'd accomplished. We'd made it as far as we could with what time we had and reconnected with Jessie, so all in all, it was not worth complaining about the lack of mileage. *But damn, I'm ready to be out of Oregon.*

The next day it took us thirty-five miles and one heck of a hill to make it from Wedderburn to the California state line, but we made it fairly early in the day. Jessie had his own cycle tour to attend to, so with a swift head nod, he took a left turn somewhere, and that was the last time we saw him. *We've kept in touch on social media but last I heard he was playing disc golf with some high-profile people across the country, but that's just rumors.*

With daylight to burn, we pushed on to a town called Fort Dick, where my immature mind would not stop imagining phallic-shaped forts everywhere. With not one priapic dwelling in sight, Geoff and I found a campground that was charging a ridiculous amount to stay the night in a tent. In keeping with tradition, we thought we would recycle the idea of stealth camping next to an overpriced campground, especially since we had successfully slept for free the night before. Being confident yet comically clamorous, we dragged our bikes through tit-high underbrush looking for a clearing. Making every twig snap and every bush rattle, we slammed our way through the woods near the costly campground, hoping to find a place where we could sleep undisturbed.

Luckily, we found a small clearing just big enough for us to sprawl out a tarp and two sleeping bags. The intensely loud, bright blue tarp took us thirty seconds to unravel. Our sleeping bags took us another minute to get laid out on the ground. In that minute and thirty seconds, a gentleman with two big dogs had silently walked up behind us.

"Y'all know you can't sleep here, right?" he said.

My lips tucked into my mouth. *Damnit.*

"Yes sir, we were just moving," I said as I shamefully picked up my sleeping bag and tarp. There was no sense in fighting it. We were caught red-handed, and it was our snowballing arrogance that had made it happen. We hadn't been trying to stealth camp; we'd been blatantly tromping around in the woods and daring someone to say something. It was a great lesson learned and one we were sure never to repeat. With our bikes tucked between our legs, we rode away in shame.

California

Holy shit! A woman with flowing silver hair just hauled ass by me on a bicycle going up this hill. She's got to be seventy years old and just demolished me. I had never been less motivated to keep pedaling.

No way. There can't be another one!? As many more cyclists came cruising past me, I finally realized a touring company was leading a trip down the West Coast at the same time as our trip. I was glad to see more cyclists, but every one of their customers passed us at blazing speeds. All of their gear was packed into a van and driven to wherever they would stop for the night. All they had to do was ride. *Why the hell are we not doing that?*

It was the first time I'd ever heard of "supported touring." *This would be a perfect place to do that! We wouldn't have to worry about finding a place to sleep after battling these hills all day. God, I would love that. Maybe I should start a company that does this on the East Coast. I could handle all the negatives of cycle touring and allow people to enjoy themselves. Hmmm... Definitely need to think about this.*

Seeing the supported tourists riding by with such ease was destroying my racing spirit, but I was still learning that cycle touring isn't always about going fast. But seeing a guy on a fixed-gear bicycle blaze by us with nothing but a tarp and a sleeping pad really put the icing on the proverbial cake. Rumors were quickly spreading up the coast among us two-wheeled vagabonds. We'd heard everything from "This is his ride north, he's already ridden all the way south" to "Well I heard he has only been riding for a week and he started in San Fran." He moved like a machine when we finally saw him, mashing the pedals so hard I heard the cranks begging him to stop.

There's no telling what this guy had truly accomplished. But I had no problem believing he was a badass after some fellow travelers told me they'd offered him a beer beside a campfire one night. They said he was so tired that he took one sip and fell off the chair onto his head, passing out from exhaustion. They pulled a tarp over him and let him sleep. That's being truly tired. When the fellow tourists woke up, expecting him to still be passed out by the fire, he was gone, already cruising up the hills and making everyone else look bad. That's discipline. That is passion.

After two days of riding in California, and with five thousand feet of elevation gain, we needed a good break. I was getting worn down mentally, and a little town called Ferndale set the stage for the moment I needed to stay motivated.

We grabbed a bite to eat at one of my top ten best burger spots of all time. It was a small shack cleverly named No Brand Burger Stand that screamed "local hole in the wall with the best food." Our stomachs led us into the parking lot, and there was no second-guessing their decision. Ten minutes later, the greasy, grass-fed, Cajun bacon burger opened every dopamine dam in my body, releasing a flood of feel-good neurotransmitters that made my body shake. My daily diet of oatmeal, peanut butter and jelly tortillas, and rice and beans was not quenching my insatiable thirst for grease. I was a crazed savage, shoveling food into my mouth by the fistful. Images of the dribbling shrimp-lip lady flashed across my mind, making me regain a semblance of composure, but it wasn't enough to slow me down.

Seconds after the last grease-laden fry disappeared, my inevitable "food coma" came on strong. I was so full that I genuinely thought about lying down right there and sleeping for the night.

"Geoff, I don't want to move, man. Let's sleep here," I said, half-joking but also dead serious.

"Nah man, let's keep going. We haven't gone that far today, and I want to get a little farther before we stop," Geoff said. He was right, too. We had only gone twenty miles that day, but the food coma combined with my bloody saddle sores ("bloody" as in actual blood and not the British term) made me insist we stay in Ferndale for the night. After a quick Google search, we found a fairground less than a mile away that looked well suited for some good stealth camping.

Riding into the fairgrounds was like riding into a scene straight out of *The Walking Dead*. Winter had shut the place down properly, and not a soul was around. Every booth was boarded up. Every tent collapsed. Every flag-less flagpole had just enough slack to clang in the wind every few seconds, just loud enough to be a dinner bell for the zombies. It was the setting for my own custom-made horror show.

I'm a bit uneasy around carnival horror, and these fairgrounds were screaming deadly clown costumes and scary carnival music.

I needed something to take my mind off the setting, so I reached for my journal in my canvas saddlebag and started writing Kaitlyn a letter. It didn't help that I was describing my precarious situation in the letter, but at least writing to her was a nice distraction to help me fall asleep. When sleep finally did come, it did not come easily. I woke at the smallest of noises all night, tossing and turning until the sun finally came up. That's when I heard the oddest sound.

Clack. Clack. Clack.

What the eff is that? Is that the dead-horse ghost nightrider guy? That's it. I'm dead.

With a total assuredness that I was going to meet my end, I opened the tent door to see my enemy.

A lone horse walked casually along the row of booths. Clack. Clack. Clack. Trotting carefree, the horse moseyed along the concrete path another hundred yards until it was out of sight. *Yep. That was creepy. It's time to go.*

We packed up and left immediately. The weirdness was enough motivation for me to ride nearly seventy miles, with little to no qualms about my bloody booty.

After a quick night's sleep on the outskirts of Benbow, California, we climbed 3,219 feet in forty miles over the most deceiving mountain I had ever seen. Every cyclist that had ridden the legendary Leggett Mountain told us the climb was, in their words, a bitch. They all said it was one of the hardest segments on the West Coast, regardless of whether they were going northbound or southbound. Geoff and I had disregarded rumors. We were confident that our mental preparation was strong enough to get us over Leggett. At least we hoped so.

The punishing climb demanded every ounce of our strength just to keep the bike moving forward. We zigzagged across the road to make the elevation gain more manageable; we mashed the pedals as hard as we could in the lowest gear, we stood up, we leaned over, and we got in the drops.

It was this mountain where my bike started to not cooperate. My front chainring would not shift down to the smallest ring without me unclipping my right foot from the pedal and manually pressing the chain with my foot while my other leg continued to pedal. Only then would the chain slide into the smallest gear and offer some relief to the punishing climb. If I forgot to manually shift into the small ring before a hill, I would have to momentarily pedal uphill with one leg. I forgot often.

From that day until the last one, I worked on fixing this problem and asked every bike mechanic we saw to look at it. It never got fixed.

Leggett was living up to the rumors and teaching me an important lesson: always listen to the people who have gone before you. My pride wouldn't let them be right, but the lactic acid in my legs and my air-deprived lungs said, "I'm sorry we didn't listen." Geoff and I tried everything to find some comfort during that climb, but nothing worked. We just settled into the burn and eventually made it to the top of the mountain. *Oh, that was it! That wasn't so bad, I mean, it sucked, but I could have done more.*

That's when Geoff and I went into our first genuinely delirious state on the trip. I'm not sure if it was a lack of water, electrolytes, food, or entertainment, but we burst into song while barreling down the mountain at top speed.

"Leggett. Leggett. You suck, you suck, Leggett.

"Leggett. Leggett. You punk. We won and won't forget it."

The meter was off, we never found the key, and the melody was to the tune of fighting feral felines in heat, but we screamed our anthem at the top of our lungs, proud of our accomplishment. Then the downhill started sloping upward again, and before we could truly relish our victory, Leggett came back for vengeance with a second mountain. Not one person had told us that the second climb existed, and they definitely didn't say that it was worse than the first. The short break between climbs had made us relax and let our guard down. My quads were blindsided by the second flood of pain. My body felt like I was drowning in a pool of liquid fire. As we struggled to the mountaintop, our song became merely a whisper.

Two thousand feet of elevation gain in twenty miles, with a ten-mile downhill between mountains... so using condensed cycling math, it's two thousand feet of climbing in ten miles. Leggett was the mountain that made us lose our minds, and I will not forget it.

Just a few miles after the second climb, the trees opened up, revealing the beautiful cliffside ocean view. It was a pedal, pedal, coast ride for a mile or so until we saw a small campground placed precariously on the cliff's edge, where we met Dale.

We set up camp, pulled out everything we needed to make dinner, and realized we didn't have any fuel for our

Jetboil. We couldn't boil water, which meant we couldn't make rice. The near flavorless, white grain had become nearly seventy percent of our caloric intake. We had peanut butter and jelly, but no tortillas. We had oatmeal too, but again, no way to boil water. *I'm going to starve. They're going to find my dry, dusty bones on this cliffside years from now and wonder what happened.*

"I'm going to see if anyone has any propane or a way for us to cook rice," I told Geoff before walking toward some other campers nearby. The first camper was a silver Airstream facing the ocean. I briefly looked around to see if anyone was home and then knocked on the front door. A gentleman named Dale answered with a suspicious look on his face. His bushy white beard, stained T-shirt, and jean shorts reminded me that even Santa Clause has an off season.

"Hey, we're on a bike tour and ran out of propane. Do you have any way we can cook rice?" I asked, not thinking it was an odd question.

He looked me up and down, eyeing my spandex shorts, and said, "Sure, come on in."

He ended up feeding us sandwiches while we listened to his wild stories about the drug runners in the California hills. The conversation made a seamless transition to his law enforcement relatives and then to his reasoning for living in an Airstream. We barely said a word, captivated by his storytelling skills. *This guy is like Walter White and Hank*

Hill smashed into one eccentric traveling thrill seeker.

As the conversation came to a close, we drank our Gatorades and washed it down with a shot of cinnamon whiskey. *Thanks, Dale.*

Two days and eighty miles later, we made it to Gualala Point Regional Park. With the sun shining through the trees and a slight breeze to cool us off, I couldn't help but acknowledge the beauty of the day, yet something was giving me an eerie feeling. We passed two enormous trees standing at the entrance as we rolled into the county campground. They looked like two towers standing watch over the campground, deciding if trespassing tourists could enter or not. The rest of the trees were only half as tall, but nearly blocked out all sunlight. We were in a bay tree forest, where the trees looked like troll's hair, a tangled mess of foliage with barely enough room to maneuver between tree trunks. It seemed like we were alone in the dimly lit campground, as opposed to the comfortable, populated, and much more sunlit road from which we'd just come. *Sure, let's go into the creepy campground, Geoff. It's cool. Whatever.*

As we pulled into the "hiker/biker" site, I noticed a sign posted on the side of a bear box. (Bear box: A wooden, sometimes metal, container used to store food, perfumes, shampoos, and other scented items so that bears don't murder the unsuspecting camper while trying to eat said camper's Honey Bun.) The sign depicted a cartoon raccoon wearing a bandit's mask and carrying bags of money in its grossly disproportionate muscular arms. "Warning: Aggressive Raccoons" was printed in bold lettering above the picture. I didn't know whether to cry from laughter or be genuinely concerned.

Finding a place to set up camp at the hiker/biker site turned out to be the night's first problem. The only clearing big enough to fit the tent with the rain fly attached was already occupied by a hipster who looked like he'd gotten there hours ago, so I had to set up the tent with one side of the rain fly down (i.e., not putting the stake in, so that half of our storage space would have the fly draped over it). Not a big deal, unless, of course, it rained, because if anything is touching the rain fly while it's wet, the water penetrates straight through.

After setting up, I glanced over to the hipster cyclist sitting at the picnic table, who'd beat us to the campsite. *That jerk stole our spot. I'm not sure why I feel entitled to it, but I do, and he took it. Character flaw number 224: Entitlement.* I pushed down any ill feelings toward the bearded man and walked over to him.

"Hey, I'm Shaun, and the guy setting up the hammock is Geoff," I said, making the first move toward awkward introductions. The man I would later remember as Mr. Run To Town gave a wave.

He was kind enough to take us on a small, informal tour of the campground.

"The bathroom is over there, the dumpster over

there… et cetera. And did you see the goofy raccoon signs?" Mr. Run To Town said, laughing. "We had better be careful!"

He loved showing us how to use his elaborate antique camping cookware. It was from the 50s or 60s and used kerosene to fuel it. There was no way it was safe or sanitary, but archaic cookware rarely ever is. With a little grooming, he would have looked like a young Walter White setting up some chemistry experiment.

I felt like a jerk. The guy was super friendly; he was just faster than us. *I'm always quick to judge. Stop doing that.*

Geoff, Mr. Run To Town, and I had a great time swapping cycling stories and sharing "the best of" places to sleep, eat, and see. He was headed north up the coast, and we were headed south, which made storytelling a necessary entertainment. Sharing stories with travelers who were headed where we had already been made the best out of their trip, and vice versa. I imagine the Oregon Trail travelers valued the same scenario: a time before Yelp told everyone where to eat. I called it Campfire Yelp. *One review, five stars. Seems legit enough to me.*

After we cooked dinner and the kerosene gases floated away, a well-groomed cyclist came rolling up to our site. With friendly hellos and an eagerness to get the conversation flowing, he introduced himself and started chatting.

I can't remember his name, but I know he was from Holland and was a history teacher there. He must have loved his job because he talked about it on multiple occasions that evening. In fact, he spoke a lot in general. But as a standard American, I was captivated by the accent and kept listening intently. Mr. Run To Town, on the other hand, was getting annoyed. He left shortly after the arrival of Mr. Holland to ride back into town for a nightcap.

As the sun started getting below the tree line, Mr. Run To Town came back with a bottle of cinnamon whiskey, which he happily passed around the communal picnic table. I wasn't particularly fond of cinnamon whiskey, but since our tour kept crossing paths with the spiced liquor, I obliged and indulged. Plus, the forest's eeriness was starting to get to me, and I figured I would need some help getting to sleep. In retrospect, I should have kept my wits about me.

It was like the raccoons were vampires, appearing at the exact moment the sun dipped below the horizon. We saw the first one about fifty yards away at another campsite. A family camping out of their car had displayed their holiday-feast-worthy food on their picnic table like an all-you-can-eat buffet. The red-and-white checkered tablecloth was covered with bread, ham, cheese, mustard, peanut butter, jelly, and any number of assorted sandwich favorites. The s'mores were elegantly laid out, ready to be roasted. Giant family-sized bags of chips were open, with a few chips falling onto the table. The father, mother, and daughter were ready to make a family memory. They never saw the vampires coming.

A loud shrill scream from their campsite made all of us whiskey-buzzed cyclists crane our necks to see what was happening. We watched in amazement as the father, with a stick in his hand, swatted at the raccoon in a valiant effort to keep the cheese thief at bay, while the mother and daughter cowered behind him. We all giggled like schoolchildren, confident that no trash panda would make us cower and hide in fear.

I got up to go dehydrate. As I walked to the restrooms, a feral hissing screech sounded by the dumpsters. I turned the corner to find two raccoons on their back legs, clawing at each other's eyes, in competition for the dumpster scraps. I laughed a bit too loud. They stopped fighting and turned toward me. I stopped laughing and slowly backed away. *This is not funny anymore.*

We were defenseless against them and decided to carefully pack up and go to bed, hoping they would leave us alone. We were naive and stupid. Minutes after getting into the tent—alone, I might add, because Geoff was bold enough to sleep in the hammock—I heard a raccoon snoop under my rain fly. *He's got my bags!* I opened the inside bug net just enough for my left hand to get a firm grasp of my pannier. I had no choice. I punched the dark-eyed dumpster kitty. He hissed back but luckily left the tent. *I've woken up with a squirrel in my tent, but I will not sleep with a raccoon. Nope.*

We listened helplessly all night as our gear got ripped

to pieces. We were victims of our own raccoon ignorance. In the morning, we assessed the damage. I peaked my head out of the tent and noticed my handlebar bag was ripped open. There were claw marks all over my bike's top tube, the bag that held our shampoo had a massive rip, and our medicine bag was tossed about in the woods. There were a few food wrappers strewn around, but all in all, it wasn't too bad. But the tipped-over, empty kitty litter bucket in the middle of the campsite confused the hell out of me.

In the middle of the night, a couple of guys named Matt and Luap had shown up. Luap, sporting a distinguished mustache and all-around hipster apparel, used kitty litter buckets as removable panniers, which I thought was a genius execution of cycle-tour mastery. But since Luap had not secured the buckets in his tent, the raccoons had knocked the bike over, ripped the bucket lids off and eaten all of the food. We felt terrible but had nothing but oatmeal to share.

As we passed the cute sign warning the campground's temporary residents of the raccoons, I couldn't help but nod my head and pay respect. They had scared the shit out of six grown men and wrecked our belongings while we'd lain in silence, listening to their claws rip apart everything we needed to survive. They'd won. I was humbled and happy to leave. *I should have used that bear box.*

The raccoons were not the only thing humbling me. I was becoming mentally fragile because of the physical toll this trip was taking on me. My body could not recover fast enough to keep tackling the hills, especially on the days after I pulled the trailer. *I really regret making that deal with Geoff. I miss using my cheap panniers every day. That trailer is infinitely more difficult to pull.* My legs were screaming the second I got on the bike that morning. Lactic acid was paying rent, in full, to live in my quads and never take a vacation. *I don't know if I'm going to make it.*

Geoff was acclimating to the discomfort much faster than I was. He could recover more quickly, which meant he was getting stronger faster. The day after the raccoon incident, I had to stop a lot. We had three decent climbs, two of which were because Geoff got us lost, really lost. I told him multiple times that we needed to stay straight on Highway 1, but he decided to take a left turn onto Coleman Valley Road that went straight up a mountain, which resulted in one thousand feet of climbing in 3.7 miles.

Geoff rode ahead, pissed off at me for disagreeing with his navigational decision. As I knowingly pedaled in the wrong direction up this mountain by myself, I watched the fog start to break. I reached the summit and rode above the clouds, seeing the sun for the first time in days. I slowly pedaled downhill, taking a moment to enjoy coasting through herds of cattle. That's when I saw Geoff heading back in my direction. He knew he was wrong, and we had suffered for it, but the beauty of the mountain was worth it. Sometimes a night can be so bad that it rolls into the next day, but eventually, things get better.

That night we met back up with Matt and Luap, who had picked up another cycle tourist named Paul. When I met the unforgettable German, he had a stern look of contemplation on his face. But once Paul started talking, he was surprisingly warmhearted. Hours went by as we swapped tour stories around the campfire, but it was during a moment away from the group, outside the men's restroom, where he gave me some life-changing advice. He said, "The mountains are the most honest thing I've ever met. Hills are lying bastards that change their minds quickly, but mountains know what they are doing. They are going up, or they are going down. They are honest." Those words have stuck with me ever since. *It's easy for me to change my mind and do something else, especially if I'm uncomfortable, but living like a mountain takes persistence and hard work. Go up or go down, but be honest.*

When Paul and I returned to the group, it had grown significantly: Mr. Run To Town had shown up, as well as an older gentleman who liked to talk a lot, and another German couple had arrived. We were a genuine pack of ragamuffins sitting around the campfire telling tour stories. The laughter was nonstop. It felt like we were all old friends reunited, until the older guy told his story.

He was part of some wilderness volunteer program that required extensive training. In the training pipeline, they were taught not to pick up tortoises. He said, "If you pick up the tortoise, it will pee and die." It got eerily awkward until Matt said, "That's it? That's all I need to know? I just graduated from tortoise school!"

Embarrassed and flustered, the older guy said in a flat tone, "You and me are about to fight." A brief silence overtook the group, and then everyone erupted in laughter.

Since that night, I have learned that the older man wasn't lying. In the desert, some tortoises survive on just two liters of water per year. And, if someone were to pick up a tortoise, it could get scared and pee. That wouldn't kill it in and of itself, but the tortoise may not be able to rehydrate before the next rainfall, and would ultimately die of dehydration. *I would never want to pee if it could be the death of me. And I'm sorry for laughing at you Turtle Man. You were right.*

We woke up to the park ranger knocking on everyone's tents, requesting to see their receipts for staying at the hiker/biker site. She said, "We only have a record of one person staying here last night, but I see at least five tents."

Yeah. Crap. I forgot.

We paid the ranger while packing up camp, waved off the other cyclists, who were already heading out for the day, and pedaled off in shame for having forgotten to pay.

It was a relatively easy day of riding, except for three extremely steep climbs, which totaled nearly three thousand feet of elevation gain. Other than that, we cruised the rest of the day, fast and with a purpose. San Francisco was just 125 miles away, and we hoped to make it there in two days. We pedaled ninety-three miles the first day, riding into Samuel P. Taylor State Park late that night. We were not picky about which site we got; we just needed a place to get horizontal and sleep.

The first, second, and third sites we found did not work because all of the trees were too big around to fit my hammock straps. Even with two hammock straps linked together, they would barely fit around the tree, which meant I would have needed four straps total to sleep in the hammock that night, and I didn't have them. *Damn beautiful redwoods.* All of the trees that I could fit my straps around were too spread out, so I decided to sleep under the stars on the ground that night and let Geoff have the tent. We picked site number four, which was as good as any other site, made rice and beans, and got ready for bed. Geoff got in the tent while I spread the tarp out, laid my sleeping pad and bag down on the tarp, then rolled the tarp around me, creating a Shaun taquito. *This will work.*

I lay there for three minutes before I heard the first one come sniffing around the trailer. *No. Not again.*

"Geoff, you hear that?" I asked.

"Yeah man, it's going to be another long night," he said.

Four minutes later, I heard the second one's paws scratch at the dirt near my tarp. I yawped, slammed open the tarp, and stood up, ready to fight every raccoon on earth. *I'm not doing this again!*

I stood in the dark for a few moments, devising a plan to rid our site of the furry bandits that I knew were staring me down from behind the treeline. An idea crashed into my mind. I went over to the trailer. I got a pack of crackers and a bottle of hot sauce. *They won't want to hang out if their mouths are on fire.*

I laid out two crackers drenched in hot sauce, rolled back into my taquito, and waited. Just minutes later, I hear a wild hiss and what sounded like a sandbag slamming onto the picnic table. *Now go away!*

The smile of victory was soon replaced with horror as I heard what was probably the victim raccoon's mafia brethren coming out of the woods.

"Geoff, move over. I'm coming in the tent," I said, with no shame in my game. I was not about to get bitten in the middle of the night. I'd rather sleep nose to nose with Geoff in his two-person tent that barely fit one small child, than to spend another night with raccoons.

We woke up the next morning, feeling lucky that the raccoons had not been aggressive like their previous counterparts and had not damaged our trailer or gear. We were ready to ride across the Golden Gate Bridge.

San Francisco

Everyone turns east eventually.

In middle school, I was always reading books about survival and primitive hunting techniques. I learned about one Native American tribe in particular that hunted deer with only a bow and arrow, even when muskets were available. They believed that deer and other large game would face east, toward the rising sun, when they were dying. Hunting with a bow was a slower death, and it gave the animal time. Time to come to terms with the inevitable. Time to fight or time to face east, lie down, and give in. I was a few days away from turning east and I needed to decide what that meant for me.

The trip so far had been a year's worth of learning, heartache, thigh cramps, and hunger pains crammed into a month, but we finally made it to San Francisco.

I've never really cared about the city. In fact, I'm not fond of big cities in general. But when I first saw the beastly Golden Gate Bridge, nothing else seemed to matter. It was a sense of accomplishment that I had never felt before. We'd made it to our first noteworthy stepping-stone. We'd made it to a bridge. A gigantic tower of metal and cables that signified we could finally rest for a few days, and then turn east.

Navigating the city was an absolute nightmare for me, but Geoff seemed at home in the bustling noise of it all. We arrived a day ahead of schedule, which never happened. Ever. But it meant that we had to kill some time and find a place to stay until our friends met up with us. Geoff had managed to make me pedal farther each day so that we could be in San Francisco at the same time as our college friends. It was never part of the plan initially, but by a striking coincidence, our friends from all around the country would be in San Francisco the same weekend as us.

We searched on Google for the cheapest hotel room near Geoff's friend's house, where we'd eventually stay. It didn't take us long to get to the hotel, and it took even less time for me to leave. I took two steps into the lobby and was ready to turn around. *Dear God, I'm so tired, but please don't let Geoff make us stay in this sketchy hotel across the street from a gloomy strip club in the middle of Chinatown.*

We approached the desk. There was an anime convention in the city, so every hotel around was price gouged. I'd never been happier to hear such an overpriced quote for a hotel room. We happily continued our tour through town, accidentally managing to take the longest route possible to the next hotel, which was still overpriced, but we stayed anyway. Clean sheets, a shower, towels, and a lamp. *Hallelujah.*

As cold as I was, my sunburned skin loved the cool water of a shower. The exfoliating soap helped remove the layers of skin cells, sweat, dirt, and Chamois Butt'r. *To anyone who has to clean this bathroom, I am sorry.*

When I finally emerged from what now looked like a mossy cave with water dripping from the ceiling, Geoff was nearly asleep on the bed, doing everything possible to watch the ending of *American Dad.* He said, "Ben, Samir, and J will be here in a bit. So will pizza." Finally, some familiar faces. And the thought of food nearly brought a tear to my eye.

Samir, a computer genius who had seemingly found the key to getting the attention of every woman in a room, was a super-tan guy with a fantastic beard. Ben Jack was the friend who always wore super fashionable shoes, usually some loafer or boot. Within the first couple of minutes of hanging out with him, I learned that he likes only soft corn tortillas, not hard shells. It's a fact that, for some strange reason, I will never forget. Then, of course, there was J, who had a tattoo on his wrist that I had asked him about when we first met. His response had made me wonder if he wanted people to ask him about it or not. So I tell everyone who might meet him to ask him about it. He was also the king of PBR. The guy drank us all under the table, and that was no easy task.

Our host in the city would be Brandon, who I had met through Geoff a few times in college. When Brandon and I first met, I scoffed at his unusual fashion sense. But after getting to know him a bit more I hated myself for judging so quickly. His personality perfectly fit his attire which I ended up admiring. Whether it was his floral button-up shirt with matching shorts or his leather jacket in the middle of summer, he was always fashionable. He also managed to perfectly match his clothes to his offbeat hair color, which on average stayed the same for about a week. The six of us were an eclectic group, ready to take on the town.

Samir, J, and Ben Jack poured into the hotel room with looks of happiness and discomfort. For J, the smell was, no doubt, overwhelming as he covered his nose with his hands as the scent struck him. I can't blame him though; our stench had penetrated all of our clothing to the point that no amount of laundry detergent would help. Our tent smelled like morning breath, our shirts like the armpits of a corpse, and our bodies radiated a general body odor that even the strongest soap couldn't penetrate, but that's the life of a cycle tourist.

After a brief moment to acclimate to the smell, they all reluctantly sat down on the bed, except Ben Jack, who felt right at home and sprawled out on the bed. It's weird, but I'm glad that he did. I hate when I invite people over, and they feel like they can't relax or touch anything.

We wasted no time lounging around and decided to go right out on the town. We walked around the city for a few hours before meeting Brandon, who came speeding up on the smallest motorized scooter I had ever seen a six-foot-tall man ride. His unbuttoned floral shirt stopped flapping in the wind behind him as he came to an abrupt stop at the curb and took a drag of his cigarette.

I realized I looked out of place when we took a panorama picture of us hanging out. The others looked like average residents of the city, while I was the only one who looked like he should be either panhandling for money, or at some Phish / Jack Johnson hybrid concert. I looked like a natural-born ragamuffin with a scraggly beard, hand-knitted beanie, capri pants, and Jesus sandals.

As we walked around San Fran, a wave of vertigo overcame me. I stopped for a second to double-check and make sure I was ok, but then I realized that it was just the odd sensation of walking that I was feeling. We walked less than a mile every day after we rode. It had only been an hour or so of walking, but it threw me off for a second. It was like getting off a boat onto dry land.

However weird the feeling was, I had to push through because I was in a new place, and whenever I travel I always make an effort to find the hole-in-the-wall restaurants and bars. Nine times out of ten, they always have the best food and atmosphere in the area. Plus, they typically don't break the bank. We spent the rest of the day, and well into the night, seeking out every dive bar in town.

On the first full afternoon of our stay, Geoff and I shook off the night before and rode out toward the Golden Gate Bridge to get some pictures and do the touristy thing. We rode through the city, stopping when we saw something cool and trying our best to see all the sights. When we neared the bridge, we rode down a side street to get a better angle for pictures underneath the bridge. Some surfers were catching two-foot waves off a jetty. I was so mesmerized by them catching such small waves that I almost didn't notice the commotion.

A group of people had gathered up on the bridge, looking over the edge. Just seconds later, an ambulance came up from behind us and went farther down the street to the water's edge.

"What happened?" I asked Geoff.

A lady next to us nonchalantly answered, "Someone jumped. It happens a lot. It's about once every two weeks."

Oh.

We tried to see if the person who'd jumped was OK, but we never found out. We left and attempted to continue enjoying the day, but the thought of someone jumping kept running through my mind. I couldn't shake the feeling off for hours.

That night, we were driving around the city with the

whole group packed into the car when we suddenly hit standstill traffic. Peering out the passenger window, I saw hundreds, if not a thousand cyclists riding down the main street.

"What is this?" I asked Brandon.

"It's Critical Mass. Everyone rides their bikes on the last Friday of the month. I'm surprised you guys didn't know about it."

Yeah. Me too! This looks fun as hell, man. The disappointment was overwhelming, but there was nothing we could do. We were an hour away from the apartment and didn't have our bikes. It almost felt like I had let the cycling community down by not riding with them. I'm not sure why I felt guilty for not attending a ride that I never knew existed, but I did.

Shrugging off the missed opportunity, we spent the next three or four days sleeping on Brandon's apartment floor and wandering around the city, eating at every pub, tapas restaurant, deli, and brewery we could find. I ate and drank calories every two hours around the clock for our entire stay. My metabolism was so high that I'm pretty sure I still lost weight.

When our time to leave San Francisco came, it was bittersweet. I was intensely ready to start riding again, having been recharged both mentally and physically, but saying goodbye to familiar faces was tough. Venturing out into the unknown, day after day, can be taxing, and I wasn't quite ready to leave my comfort zone again.

It took us longer than usual to pack up our gear, but we finally managed to scrounge it up from around the apartment. I happily helped Geoff attach the trailer to his bicycle, knowing I would never have to pull it again. We had made an agreement to tour with the gear we'd bought, which meant Geoff would always pull the trailer and I would use the panniers. We straddled our bikes on the sidewalk, said goodbye to everyone, and started pedaling again. It felt a lot like leaving Dave and Ashley in Oregon. It was our second start to the tour and one that meant a lot more to me than the first. This time I was turning east and riding toward who I wanted to be with, instead of riding away from my unhealthy relationships. From here on, my tour was about growth and my decision to not live in the past anymore. I was now riding toward the rising sun.

Vallejo

Very rarely do I get scared, but there are three things that will turn my stomach to knots. The first is entirely rational: clowns. When I was entirely too young, my friend next door said to come over and watch a movie. I was super excited when I saw him sneaking the VHS tape out of his mom's movie cabinet and running upstairs. I quickly followed him, and we began watching *Stephen King's It*, the scariest, most age-inappropriate television I had ever seen. So, being afraid of clowns makes sense.

My second fear is dogs. I have been chased and run down by more dogs than I can count, probably because I run and bike a lot. Also, I'm not that fast, so the dogs usually win. So in my mind, my top two fears are perfectly logical.

My third fear does not make much sense. It makes

me so uneasy, that I feel the need to test my fear repeatedly to make sure it hasn't happened. I am terrified of being paralyzed, unable to use any limb, and being bed-bound for the rest of my life. It scares me to death, so much that I push my body as hard as I can for as long as I can, even when it's a terrible idea.

For instance, one summer, I was in the early stages of training for a half-marathon. The farthest distance I had run in practice was six miles. Well, I had a bad knee pain near the end of another six mile run one day, so I called Reid, my other high-school best friend, and got him to ride his bike beside me while I finished my six miles. I got to the six-mile mark and felt a fear that I had injured my leg and would never again be able to use it. *Completely irrational, I know.* I decided to redo the six-mile loop to make sure my leg was working.

I finished the loop and then did it again.

I was on the 15th mile when my leg quit working. The pain was radiating throughout my leg and into my back. I had to lay down in the middle of the country road for about two hours before the pain subsided enough for me to walk home. Reid offered to leave and get help multiple times, but I needed to work through my pain on my own. I tend to push myself too hard out of fear that I won't be able to one day.

I've never asked him, but apparently, Geoff does the same thing.

We had just gotten off the ferry that connects San Francisco to Vallejo when the heatwave smacked us straight in the face. When we'd gotten on the boat in San Francisco, it had been in the high sixties. Somehow, as if we had passed through some weather twilight zone, when we got off the short ferry ride, there was a heat index of 108, and we were not ready for it. At all. It was so hot that my eyes hurt; not even blinking helped. Before we had mounted our trusty steeds, I had already downed what little water I was carrying, with little forethought of what was to come.

The more suburban town of Vallejo was a welcome sight for me. Bigger cities tend to stress me out a bit too much since I try to pay attention to even the smallest details. It becomes too overwhelming. But in Vallejo, I was able to slow down a bit and enjoy my time. Geoff, on the other hand, was not enjoying his time. It was just a mile down the street before Geoff was sweating way too much and working way harder than he should have been. He was pushing his body hard, working through the pain, and doing his best to keep going. *He's afraid of giving up.*

I've always loved the heat and tend to feel much more comfortable in it than most people, probably because my mom would want to save money in the summer by not using the AC. Growing up, my friends wouldn't come over because my house was too hot, which I can't blame them for. I would go outside into the southern heat for a reprieve from the house. But at least now, my tolerance for heat works to my advantage.

We made it eight miles down the road to a street that paralleled Highway 80 when Geoff had to pull over. We were on a moderately challenging climb, so I figured he just wanted a break.

Breathing heavily, Geoff said, "Dude. Something's not right. I'm not feeling too good."

"OK. We can chill here for a bit, under this tree. You need some water?" I asked.

"Yeah, you got some?" he said.

I shook my empty water bottle. *Uhhh...* "I thought maybe you had some in the trailer I could get you," I said, trying to recover from my empty offer.

Geoff lay, silent, on the side of the road for the better part of thirty minutes. He was barely sweating at all, his skin was flushed, and he was extremely irritable. *I've got to find a place to stay around here. He can't be riding like this.*

I walked up and down the street four hundred yards in either direction, and the best place I could find was a mattress in a ditch on the side of the road. Lying around the bedding were ripped up magazines, which could have been adult in nature, empty beer cans, and a blanket. *If it's good enough for some homeless guy, it's good enough for me.*

"Hey man, we can sleep here for the day until the sun goes down and then ride a bit farther to get something to drink," I said, mildly confident he wasn't going to go for my genius plan.

"I'm not sleeping on a mattress in the street!" he yelled.

Whoa. OK, buddy. Calm down. The mattress is in the ditch. I would never sleep on a bed in the street.

I gave up trying to help him and just let him work through it on his own. During his suffering, I chose to relax a bit and read some more of my current book, *The Giver* by Lois Lowry. Throughout the trip I read only short, classic novels because I didn't want to carry around heavy books that would slow me down, and that I couldn't guarantee I would finish before my ride ended. In total, I read *White Fang, Hatchet, The Giver,* and *Civil Disobedience* before switching to audiobooks.

Geoff eventually managed to get back on his bike, and we made it to Cordelia, where we properly hydrated and refueled our bodies. *Hmm. I guess a months' worth of PBR crammed into seven days isn't the best thing for hydration.*

A Gatorade and some crackers must have hit the spot, because Geoff was ready to ride again fairly quickly. Luckily, we had virtually no elevation gain and rode another forty miles to Davis, California, where Geoff insisted we get a hotel room.

The next morning, Geoff and I made an agreement to be patient with each other and let our bodies guide the tour. Geoff had truly needed a night in a hotel, no doubt. He had been in a bad spot physically and needed a good night's sleep. But now we both wanted to get "back to our roots" and start touring the way we'd initially set out doing, camping outdoors.

We both wanted to cruise through the upcoming city of Sacramento as fast as we could, so we had no temptations to stay in another hotel. As we crested a hill and saw the city's impressive skyline, we passed a bus stop where an older man sat, maybe in his late fifties with a scruffy beard and corn-colored teeth. He took his cane, held it in the air, and yelled, "I'll stick this in your spokes!" Normally, that would have been alarming, but I was too distracted by his outfit. I swear this man was wearing a Girl Scout uniform with the beret and all. Geoff swears it was a kilt with a sash, but I've bought enough cookies to know it was a Girl Scout uniform. It will forever be a debate between Geoff and me.

Regardless of the man's attire, the encounter was unsettling, and once we no longer saw any kilted men, we pulled over to try and find a route that didn't take us down into the heart of Suckramento. We found the American River Bike Trail, which would take us through the entire city without ever having to deal with traffic, noise, or people with canes. Once we'd navigated to the trail, however, we did have one incident I'd never planned on.

We were slowly coasting along the winding trail, checking out the river and enjoying our time away from the city buildings, when we rounded a blind corner and saw a coyote just off to the side of the path. He was no more than fifteen feet away, hunched down on his rear legs with his back arched, fearlessly displaying his teeth and making a weird growling noise. I pedaled faster to get past him. Geoff slowed down. *Oh man, this is so much worse than a dog.* When I stood up on my pedals to get some leverage, the coyote stopped arching his back. He stopped showing his teeth and became silent. *What? What's he doing?*

He trotted off into the woods, leaving only one thing behind. Poop.

We made it to Folsom City before finding a place to stealth camp near Folsom State Prison. Standing on a hill that overlooked the prison, with the setting sun making the sky a bright orange, I took a moment to appreciate my freedom. I wasn't tied to my cell phone or busy checking social media. I didn't have to stress about being late to work. I was completely untethered to the "real world." I took a deep breath and appreciated the moment.

I lulled myself to sleep singing "Ring of Fire."

Cooks Station

From Folsom City, we planned to make it to Cooks Station in one day, but the hills destroyed our morale and, more importantly, our legs. Not being able to push the pedals at ninety rotations per minute (the optimal cadence for cycling), even in the smallest gear, took its toll on my pride. Not being able to get what seemed like five rotations per minute was absolute mental agony! *I should be able to do this by now! What's going on?!* I was frustrated with myself and with the lack of forward motion. It was only later that I learned we'd been trying to take on eight thousand feet of total elevation gain in fifty-six miles.

In addition to the chest-pounding, leg-pumping climb, the traffic was another big player in the war against our morale. Curvy, narrow roads with rowdy, high-school scholars do not mix well with touring bicyclists. On more than one occasion, coming up to a blind turn, the driver of a two-door, beat-up pickup truck with a lift kit would slow down to a near stop. Once they made it right beside us, they would put the gas pedal to the floor, burning out and achieving a grandiose display of attempted manhood. *Congratulations, you're an idiot.*

Cooks Station was our plan because we expected it to have a luxurious campground. However, we severely underestimated the "mountain tax." (Mountain tax: A tax, paid in calories, that is directly proportional to elevation gain and power generated.) The road to Cooks Station pointed straight up the mountain.

As I continued internally griping about the road, I looked around for a place to stop for the night. We were so far behind the day's loosely defined goal, there was no use in pushing further to reach Cooks Station. As I wiped the sweat off my forehead, I caught a glimpse of a gap between the trees. The road had a sharp drop-off to the right, and with the tops of every tree at near eye level and butted up against themselves, the gap was glaringly obvious. The cliff, just four feet away from the side of the road, prevented anyone from seeing how far down it went or what lay at the bottom. *That could be a perfect place to sleep.* We stopped and I hopped off my bike, handing it to Geoff to hold while I went down the hill. A perfect clearing opened up at the bottom that was invisible from the road. The disappointing day had been exhausting, so we welcomed the secret spot, hoping we could sleep and finish up the rest of the mountain tomorrow.

Standing on the roadside, Geoff lowered my bicycle down the drop-off. At the bottom was a dark, well-concealed clearing just ten feet away from the road. It was like someone planted the trees in a perfect circle, leaving just enough room for two sleeping bags to sprawl out in the middle. With the sun going down and the thick tree shade, it was getting harder to see, but the ground was spongy and soft, urging me to lay down and rest up.

As I rolled out the tarp, which would be my bed for the night, I couldn't help but think of my favorite game growing up: hide and seek. I loved when my family would have a get-together with the next-door neighbors and all the kids were thrown out of the house while the adults played cards and drank their laughing drinks. The entire gang of neighborhood hoodlums were forced to stay outside, so we did what any bored 90s kid would do: we played either kick the can or hide and seek. I always voted for hide and seek, mostly because of my love for two moments that would happen, the first being the countdown. The person designated "it" would always, with no warning, turn their head and begin counting. Adrenaline would immediately fill my veins as I'd sprint to the spot where they would "never find me." Secretly I hoped to get caught, but not before watching "it" search for the other hiding targets.

The second reason I always voted for the game was for the sudden dash out of my hiding spot toward the safe zone once "it" was too close. That explosion of leaves and debris, coming from behind my feet as I sprinted with everything I had, never failed to be the most exciting part of the game.

I had the same feeling when hiding in the ditch beside Highway E16. Excited and nervous that someone could spot us so easily, but not caring because I was too tired and cocky. I knew if someone did find us, the explosion of leaves and debris would follow—although what form it would take, I wasn't sure. I couldn't stop running the countless scenarios of what could happen and how I would react. I smiled because no matter what, I knew that I had a plan, and I would respond. *This trip has at least taught me that much.*

Just before bedtime, we noticed nearly a hundred scorpion holes surrounding us. They were everywhere. How had I not seen them when we first laid out our bags? *Great, I'm sleeping next to death. No wonder the ground was so spongy. I dare one of these things to sting me. I've watched Fear Factor. I will eat you. Hello California, you bastard.* I tried to push the thoughts of scorpion stings out of my mind by taking stock of our situation.

We were not optimistic about the hills.

We were tired.

We were sore.

We would finish.

The next morning as we packed up, we watched a cyclist climb up the mountain, just above our heads. He was "cheating" by riding from the right to the left side of the road, making each pedal stroke easier but making the day and hill much slower. It was nothing Geoff and I hadn't done in Oregon, but we were now trying to take the mountains head-on. We were committed to riding the mountain as prescribed. He never saw us. Never knew we were ten feet off the side of the road. For the rest of the day, I looked off of every ledge, under every bridge, and behind every wall we passed, looking for stealth campers.

Cooks Station turned out to not be the luxurious camping spot we thought it would be. Sitting at an elevation of five thousand feet, Cooks Station was little more than a gas station with a small diner inside. The red and white checkered tablecloths, wood-paneled walls, and spiral staircase leading downstairs reminded me of a diner from a Stephen King novel. It was a cozy place, especially with the wood-burning stove, but I was getting a weird vibe from it. Why we thought it would have a good place to camp, I have no idea, but there we were, exhausted and hungry.

I never got the lady's name who was working behind the counter, but I will always remember her. She was a shorter lady who wore glasses and spoke like a muppet, and I could have listened to her for hours. We kicked up a conversation about our trip and told her we were looking for a place to stay.

"You can sleep out back if you want," she offered. *Well, that was easy enough.* We thanked her and continued talking about Cooks Station.

"Oh yeah," she said in her Kermit-like voice, "this place is for sure haunted."

Skeptical, but interested, I took the bait. "Yeah? How do you know?"

"A bunch of people have seen a woman standing at the top of that spiral staircase there. I've only heard her a few times, but she wanders around here at night and early in the mornings," she said, obviously convinced that her story was the truth. I'm not a believer in ghosts, but I'm not a disbeliever either, so there's plenty of room for me to get shivers down my spine at a good ghost story. *Well, good thing we are sleeping outside.*

After a quick bite to eat at the diner, we set up camp behind the gas station. Before we could get the tent completely set up, bees started showing up out of nowhere. This was not a swarming, pissed-off hive, but probably a couple of hundred yellow jackets flying around, just curious enough to make me uneasy. The noise of them buzzing by was so loud that I couldn't focus on setting up the tent. We stopped setting up camp, and I went back inside to ask if there was another location where we could stay, to avoid the bees.

"Oh, they're just meat bees," she said, as if I had any idea what she was talking about.

145

"I think they're yellow jackets," I replied.

"No. They are meat bees."

"OK," I said, "what does that mean?"

She pulled out a pack of bacon and said, "Just put a couple of pieces a hundred yards away from your camp. I promise you won't see another bee."

OK, this is a new one for me. We did as she said, and sure enough, the meat bees left us alone for the rest of the day. A bacon sacrifice for a peaceful night's sleep... the irony was not lost on me.

Carson Pass

There was no question, the road up to Cooks Station was hard. We'd struggled, the random cyclist who'd passed us in the morning had struggled, and I'm sure even the animals struggled to walk around. The area is just mountains: beautiful, serene, and the hardest things I have ever had to ride.

The day after Cooks Station was turning out to be no different from the day before. We were just a few pedal strokes into the day's ride and already needed a break to chug some water. Geoff checked Google, attempting to justify the difficulty of this ride and put his mind at ease. We learned that from Somerset to Cooks Station had been a net elevation difference of three thousand feet, which felt like quite the accomplishment. (We would later learn that we had climbed a total of eight thousand feet, which made me feel much better.) After our water break, we got back on our bikes and resumed the slow grind up the mountain. That was when the clouds opened up, a beam of light shone directly down on Geoff and I, and God himself said, "Now climb it all again."

Carson Pass sits at 8,574 feet, three thousand feet higher than Cooks Station, plus another 574 feet up just for fun. When I saw that on the map, my heart sank. *There is no way I can climb like that again. I can barely walk today.* Sure, three thousand feet isn't that bad when adding up all the little ups and downs of the whole day, but this was not total elevation gain; this was the net difference in elevation between towns, or in our case, gas stations. I knew that that meant today could very well be another five or eight or even ten thousand feet of climbing. I was mentally beaten before the day even began, and nothing could bring me out of my emotionally destitute slump. I did not want to move.

"Alright, let's get going," Geoff said.

Don't sound so eager to suffer. We will get there eventually.

Every time I put Janice (my bike's name that she earned on Carson Pass) between my legs the day after a long ride, it was painful. Not just uncomfortable, but painful. I was riding the stock saddle, and to put it nicely, it felt like I was sitting on a broken glass bottle all day.

Ouch. Let's start the day.

It was nothing but sweat, neck pain, and butt rash while climbing all day with the sun in my eyes. Every day seemed to be blending into the next one. Wake up, ride, sleep, and that was it, but the ride up to Carson Pass felt different. I remember the air feeling clean and light, with the sun shining through the clouds like the dreamy romantic scene of an indie movie. It made the whole day, including all the inconveniences, easier. But like most low-budget movies, it came to an abrupt end, and then it was time to find a place to sleep.

The sun sank below the horizon, making it hard to see. Luckily Geoff is half-blind, and I'm as picky as a middle school boy looking for his first kiss, so finding places to sleep in the dark was easy. It was when Geoff could see where we were sleeping that made it difficult.

"You ready to sleep, dude?" I asked. "I don't care where we stop; we can finish the mountain tomorrow and have an easy day. Plus, I don't want to go bombing down a mountain in the dark. It got a bit sketchy last time." I hated having to dodge those potholes and broken glass, while cars whizzed by within inches.

"OK. How about here?" Geoff asked.

It could have been a dumpster, and I would have slept in it, but Geoff had spotted a small, runaway-truck ramp on the opposite side of the road that topped out to an almost flat campsite, where we could see the occasional car passing below us, just off the ridge. It was the perfect spot, almost like people had stayed there before. We hung our food from a tree away from the campsite so that bears wouldn't get into it. The raccoon incidents were all too fresh in our minds.

Around 3 AM, a truck rolled up about fifty yards from us on the other side of the hill from the ramp. I saw only their headlights shining above the tent, but I didn't think they saw us. I heard them get out and rustle around the bed of their truck, but I had almost zero regard for safety when it came to sleep, so I ignored the new arrival and immediately passed back out.

When I did finally wake from the dead, Geoff was already up and cooking breakfast. The smell of boiling water and hydrated oats did nothing to stir my soul. I slowly meandered out of the tent with zero motivation to get on the bike.

"How did you not wake up?" Geoff said.

Rubbing my eyes to get the sleep out, I replied, "I did, but I didn't really care if they saw us or not."

"Bro, we were being hunted!"

"What?" My mind raced to *The Most Dangerous Game*.

"Yeah, they parked at the bottom of the hill and heard deer antlers banging together, so they started stalking the noise. The guy was super excited cause he's never been so close to anything like that. Then they heard the deer rustling around on the ground and were going to shoot them when they noticed the tent flapping. The antler noise they heard was our food banging around in the tree, and the rustling was us rolling in our sleeping bags. We were almost shot in our sleep!"

"What? How did you find this out?" I asked.

"When I got up this morning, he was standing by his truck, so I went to talk with him. He said we should be more careful with where we sleep 'cause this is public hunting grounds."

Well, I guess anyone pulling over on the side of the road in the middle of the night is a bit sketchy, including ourselves. The whole time Geoff was talking, I was trying to figure out what he was doing with the bike trailer's tube. It looked like he was patching it, but I knew we were out of glue. We'd cut open the glue tube the last time we'd used it, a few days ago, to scrape out the remaining bit, and we hadn't seen anything resembling a bike shop since.

"What are you doing with the tire?" I asked.

"Patching it," he said with a slight grin. "When I woke up I saw that the trailer tire was flat so I cut the bark off that pine tree and used the sap to glue the patch on."

I laughed at the ingeniousness of it. I'm pretty good at repurposing or making do with what I have, but I would never have thought of that. I've heard of using a dollar bill to fix a blowout on a tire's sidewall, but using sap to patch a tube? It certainly made me reevaluate what we needed to bring with us versus what we thought we needed.

Carson Pass

It was time to summit Carson Pass. This peak was going to be the highest mountain I had ever cycled. It took us about thirty minutes and a thousand more feet of elevation gain, but we cruised to the top of Carson Pass full of energy, excited, and thankful not to have been shot. At some point during the trip, Geoff and I decided to do something we named "push-downs," which is exactly like a push-up, but instead of our bodies moving through the air, we push the earth down. It was a goofy change of perspective that helped us enjoy summiting the mountains all the more. We did one push-down for every hundred feet of elevation.

Lying face down at the top of Carson Pass, under the clear sky and breathing the oxygen-deficient air, we did 85 push-downs to celebrate our accomplishment. We felt like kings of the mountain, if only for a second.

I barely had to touch the pedals over the next thirty-six miles. It was one of the most epic downhills of my life, with a 7-foot total elevation gain and a 3,914-foot total elevation loss. The trees thinned out, the rock faces disappeared under the rolling hills, and unremarkable shrubs covered the landscape. The entire ecosystem changed in an hour. *It's so much easier to breathe down here.*

Nevada

Changing lanes, an angry old man honked three times and gave us the stink eye. Ten minutes later, a heckler yelled out of his window at us. On the eastern side of Carson Pass and over the California state line, we rode with a newfound feeling that somehow we were wrong for riding bicycles. Nevada was proving to be quite an unwelcoming state.

On the way out of Carson City, just as we got on the "loneliest road in America," we passed a slew of "bunny ranches," a perfect place for truckers and others to find the company of women for a price. Is it a coincidence that brothels and the loneliest road in America are next to each other? Probably not, but we decided to keep riding through the dusty town, opting not to risk catching anything other

154

than a flat tire.

It seemed like stopping to patch the inner tubes on our tires was becoming an everyday occurrence. Nevada, and the West in general, was absolutely brutal on our tires. Every stop we made to fix a tire frustrated at least one of us, if not both, to the point where it would take hours to calm down, or in my case, until the next time we ate. We made camp at a dam reservoir near Fallon, Nevada, shortly after the fourth flat on the trailer occurred.

Geoff and I had been getting along better recently, but it seemed the morale between us ebbed and flowed like the mountains we were crossing. We could have a good laugh one minute and pass sharp looks the next. The tension was annoyingly painful. And the communication between us was breaking down and making every day harder.

It all came to a head at the summit of the second climb for the day. We got off our bikes, and Geoff asked, "OK, so how many push-downs for this one?"

It was an honest question, but his tone insinuated that he disagreed with the number we'd decided on earlier in the day.

"Sixteen. Remember?" I said in a harsh tone.

Speaking over my answer, he said, "Because I'm not doing forty-six. We didn't start at sea level."

"I know," I said, shaking my head in annoyance.

"What's your problem?!" he exclaimed, finally reaching his breaking point.

"You've had sharp comments all day, man! Calm down."

"No I haven't!" he said over his shoulder as he bent down to pick up his bike.

From the push-up position, I watched Geoff mount his bike and start to take off. There was no point in doing push-downs for this hill. It was supposed to be fun, but clearly, we were not in the mood for fun. I got on my bike and began to leave, but Geoff was already a hundred yards ahead and moving much faster than me. *I hate these pointless fights.*

I hung my head and stared at the ground while I coasted down the hill. The small fight had me breathing heavily, plus I wasn't used to the new elevation yet. *It seems like I'm always breathing heavy. Why is it so hard to pedal?! I can't believe I'm getting tired on a downhill. Are my brakes misaligned?* As I struggled to keep moving down the hill, I bent down to move my brake pads. *No. That's not it.* I looked between my legs to make sure nothing was stuck in my gears. *No. That's not it either. What the heck is going on?!* That's when I noticed the bulge in my tire at the bottom of the rim.

A thorn had pierced my rear tire at the worst possible moment. Geoff and I were at each other's throats, and now I had to change my tube. *Change my tube?! Geoff has all the tools! Shit!*

I stopped riding and threw my bike into the sand as if somehow, acting like a child would make my situation better. Nope. The tire was still flat. Geoff was way out of shouting distance with no cell service. The tools were with him, and I was on the loneliest road in America. I had only seen one car all day!

I can't just sit here. Geoff's pissed, and I know he's not going to look back for miles. I picked my bike up out of the sand and used my backup hand pump to blow up my tire. I could hear the air leaking from the tube. I rode four hundred yards as fast as I could, watching as my rim moved closer to the ground and Geoff moved further away into the desert heat.

Dismount bike.

Pump tire.

Ride hard.

Rinse and repeat.

I must have done that six or seven times. My arms and legs were pumped full of blood. My heart was slamming out of my chest. I knew I couldn't keep doing this forever, but what other choice did I have? I had to catch him or at least close the distance. Finally, an SUV passed. I must have looked frantic while waving him down because he abruptly stopped.

"Thanks for stopping," I said in between gasps of air.

"No problem," he said. It was a middle-aged man with bumper stickers of national parks and race distances like "26.2" and "13.1" on his car. An outdoor enthusiast, who was currently dressed like a businessman.

"Can you tell my buddy to come and help me out?

I've got a flat tire, and he has all the tools. He should be just ahead, pulling a yellow trailer."

"Sure. No problem. What kind of car is he driving?"

"This kind," I said, pointing to my bike.

He laughed pretty hard and nodded. "OK, I'm sure I can catch him," he said with a smirk.

"Thank you. You're truly saving me right now."

"No problem," he said and drove away.

I sat in the middle of the high desert for what felt like an eternity. It was so quiet that I could hear the blood rushing around in my head and my heart beating against my ribs. There were no leaves to rustle and nothing for the wind to stir against, just pure silence. For a second, as I lay on the side of the road with my eyes closed, I thought I heard someone in a tracksuit slowly walking toward me, but when I opened my eyes, I saw only a bird circling above me about four hundred yards in the air, flapping its wings. *A bird flying sounds like a tracksuit. Things I've never thought about for $300, Alex.*

Geoff finally came back. He had stopped a mile or so down the road and was waiting for me when the SUV pulled up, letting him know I was stranded. While I fixed my first flat, he made a PB&J tortilla.

The reality of our situation hit home that day. We were dependent on each other to make it across. We'd started together, and we needed to finish together. Without ever speaking about the fight, our communication got better, and so did morale. Sometimes it takes nothing more than a small thorn to be humbled.

Hippies And Hot Springs

It is not uncommon as a vagabond cyclist to find oneself bonking (bonking: when all energy stores are long gone, and the mind is begging the body to keep going) at the top of a mountain. It is, however, quite unfortunate to have bonked at the bottom of an upcoming mountain. That was my status near Austin, Nevada. My muscles were laughing at me. *You can't make it. Austin is too far away, and you are exhausted.* It was true, Austin was miles away and all uphill, but we were running out of water and had to make it. Also, it was getting dark quickly, and after a close call with a boisterous fellow in a truck a few nights earlier, I wanted off the road by nightfall.

If the road had taught me anything up to this point, it was time to "nut up or shut up" as Woody Harrelson in the movie *Zombieland* would say. If a three-mile-an-hour pace was all I could manage, then that's what would happen. Sometimes putting my head down and hoping my legs would move was enough because somehow, eventually, I always made it.

It was not an epic finish to the day. We rode at a blistering two miles per hour up one thousand feet of elevation over three miles to Austin, finishing well after nightfall. Luckily, we found a grassy area behind the city's public pool and made camp. *I never want to ride my bike again.* Whether it was because of the day or an empty belly, I was defeated. I was exhausted, and by no elementary definition of the word, either. I was done. To make matters better, Geoff was sharing in my agony. I did not enjoy watching Geoff suffer, but if he was perky or lighthearted and I was miserable, a level of extreme envy appeared that could quickly turn to annoyance, then anger. But at that moment, Geoff and I shared a collective feeling of misery. Teamwork.

"I am not getting on my bike. Let's walk to the diner."

"No joke. I couldn't ride if I wanted to."

It doesn't matter who said what because we were both thinking it. We walked to the diner for a much needed dose of cheap, high-fat, and covered-in-grease food. The meal lifted our mood instantly. To add the cherry on top, the server at the diner told us about some hot springs on the other side of the mountain. *Day off. Day off. Day off!* I knew that nothing would stop me from spending the next day soaking in natural hot springs before the server even finished talking.

We went directly from the diner into a gas station for dinner number two. On the way, we saw two ragged-looking cyclists who appeared nearly as tired as we did. I was giddy and eager to ask where they came from, how many miles per day they were doing, and several other questions that get asked anytime touring cyclists meet. A postcard with the answers could be printed out and handed to save time, but it's not as fun.

I felt a bit of an awkward vibe in the air as I asked these questions and realized that they were not reciprocating with similar questions, or any questions at all. *Are they just rude or pretentious?* Why was this conversation different from the countless ones before? The answer came to me when I saw the bewildered look on their faces. I was wearing my "street" clothes. This is not to say I looked normal, because the green three-quarter pants and striped black-and-gray V-neck made me look like a homeless person or a poor hipster, both of which I may have resembled, but certainly not a cyclist. They had no idea that Geoff and I were on the same adventure they were. When I'd asked where they were sleeping that night, they'd understandably put their guard up.

That was how we met Tom and Yaris.

Yaris was from England, and from my first impression, I learned that the Englishman loved gas station bean burritos and oversized face-covering scarves.

Tom was from New Jersey. I questioned how serious a cycle tourist he was when I noticed his saddle's nose pointed nearly straight down. When I mentioned something about it to him, he was nearly as shocked as I was.

"Damn, I didn't mean to tilt it that much," Tom said. "It was riding me pretty hard up the mountain, 'cause I like to ride in the drops, so I tilted the nose a bit, but damn, I didn't mean to do that." He laughed with either embarrassment or humility. Either way, the realization made all tensions fall to the wayside, and an immediate bond formed between the four of us.

We invited them to stay in our cozy nook behind the public swimming pool for the night. It was not often that Geoff and I had information to offer because we were always rolling into a town late at night, so whenever I knew of a free place to stay or a cheap place to eat, I shared it, even if no one wanted to hear it. This made conversations a bit weird sometimes, but whatever. I was happy to share and, in doing so, made two fantastically fearless friends. Campfire Yelp at its finest.

Tom and Yaris had met in Chicago and been riding together, apart from a short stint in the Midwest, up until that point. To the best of my memory, Yaris began his tour somewhere around Pennsylvania with nothing but a compass to guide him, while Tom started his tour around New

Jersey. Their stories of Kansas made me grateful that it was not on our route. Blistering headwinds in every direction, nothing but rolling hills, and very little shade the entire time were just a few of the highlights of the state. *No thank you.*

The entire time we were sharing information about our respective tours, Tom's mohawk and carefree attitude kept me questioning, is this guy screaming for attention or genuinely cool? After realizing the ridiculous number of similarities between him and myself, I concluded that he was a naturally cool person. Unless I was attention-hungry; then my entire worldview would be shattered, but that was another issue. *Character flaw number 229 (in review): Am I attention-hungry?*

The camp that night consisted of Yaris's mummy tent, Tom's Hennessy hammock, and Geoff and my "two-person" tent. There was already a feeling of community among us as we collectively struggled to find a place to set up Tom's hammock. With nothing but a wall of dirt on one side of us, two trees twenty yards away from each other, and a chain-link fence that paralleled the dirt wall, there was no perfect combination of hammock hanging apparatus. Tom somehow made it work, as I'm sure it was not his first time. After we set up camp, we sat on the cold, wet grass to eat a second supper and trade more tour stories. My favorite story about Yaris was when he almost burned his tent down with his camp stove because he cooked inside his tent to warm himself up. He managed to put the fire out, but not before a large hole burned into the top of his tent. *Don't try to get warm by bringing the camp stove inside the tent. Check.*

The next morning, after a night of trading hilarious and informative tour stories (which consistently turned out to be my favorite kind of night), we packed up and began saying our goodbyes, during which I managed to step in coyote feces. The smell has attached itself to my memory of the moment, and I can't seem to think of one without the other. After scraping the coyote surprise out of my bike shoe's cleat, which took a bit of precision so as not to fling the unwanted present everywhere, I realized that for me to be in this predicament, a coyote must have been present at some point during the night. The poop had not been there when we went to sleep. The coyote must have snuck into our camp during the night. *Nevada is wild.*

On that temperate-weather morning, we took a group photo, saddled up, and had just begun heading out when I asked, "Are y'all sure you don't want to go to the hot springs with us? You know you could use a day off and someone new to talk to." I enjoyed Geoff's company but the extrovert in me screamed for new conversations.

With a big grin on his face, Yaris said, "Ah, I would enjoy a good soak in the springs."

Tom, shaking his head, smiling, said, "Let's do it."

They both knew that going to the hot springs meant they would have to climb the back side of the mountain they had climbed the night before and then re-climb the first side to net a total of zero miles closer to their goal. True adventurers. Unfortunately for them, when they decided to go to the hot springs, there was not a cloud in the sky. By the time we got to the top of the mountain, the scene had changed. Drastically.

Fifteen hundred feet of climbing while getting pelted with sleet, battling winds that pushed us into oncoming traffic, and enduring temperatures that made ice cream look warm. That was the challenge; the hot springs were the reward. It was so uncomfortable, so miserable, that I started laughing. I didn't even mind as the cold rain made its way down the collar of my jersey onto my neck and within minutes soaked me to the core. Tom and Yaris had just ridden this mountain last night, and they were doing it again in a sleet storm, all for the hopes of finding some hot springs in the middle of the frigid desert. Hysterical laughter broke out among everyone.

The server at the diner had told us that after we summited the mountain, we needed to go down a short gravel road. *Oh, it's just four hundred meters down the road, they said. It's not that far, they said. They lied.* The dirt road, which beat our tires to near death, was six miles long. Not only was it still sleeting on us, but we also couldn't ride fast because of the gravel. Topping out at four miles per hour on a road that resembled the surface of Mars, it took what seemed like days of bone-shaking riding to get there.

How much longer? I stared at the ground, trying to

zone out and just ride to pass the time. I briefly looked up to see if I could lay eyes on the hot springs. A topless woman, partly hidden behind the rolling hills, bent down and disappeared behind the leafless bushes. *I've been out here too long. What did I just see?*

I tried not to stare, but I knew I had seen something and I needed to make sure I wasn't losing my mind. We crested a small hill and there she was, with four other less-than-dressed hippies, hanging out in a hot spring the size of a large jacuzzi. I looked around at the area and saw a few other hot springs, but they all looked dirty and unmaintained. The occupied spring was the cleanest, so we waited our turn and instead of hopping right in, we made some lunch and tried to warm up.

The naked hippies made all four of us uneasy; after all, I don't think any of us had seen four nude people in a pool of naturally heated water. To break the unsettling tension, I walked over to the one I perceived as the "lead hippie" and I introduced myself. In the middle of our introduction, he stood to get out of the pool and put on a towel. Every bit of me was shaking from the cold, and this man was only wearing a towel. I couldn't wait to get into the steaming water. He then continued the introduction while walking over to their van and grabbing a small cloth bag. As we continued making small talk, he walked to a nearby spring, bent down to dig a small hole in the dirt and started planting some type of seed that he pulled from the bag.

Most people struggle to maintain eye contact during conversation, but he managed to continue proper introductions, plant a seed, and not freeze to death. I was curious about what he was planting and why.

He told me, in incredible detail, about the native edible plants that grew around the area. The group would travel around in a very well-thought-out pattern, which allowed them to eat what they had planted around the state. I loved how this group of people lived in a van, eating only what they planted. It was yet another glimpse into a lifestyle I'd never thought of. This trip was exposing me to a side of America I'd never known existed, challenging my way of thinking.

As the hippies filed into their van, we cyclists took a soak in the springs and began to laugh at all we had gone through to get there. It was a hilariously miserable day, but that moment made everything worth it. So much better that we took another day off to fully enjoy the natural benefits of a long sulfur bath.

That night, as Tom, Yaris, Geoff, and I sat around the campfire talking about home, the second wave of storms came. We didn't care. As touring cyclists, we always have a community and a family on the road. We were freezing, hungry, and home. The fireball whiskey and sense of family warmed our hearts while the cheap beer warmed our bodies.

The next morning we rode back down the six-mile

gravel road and stopped when the gravel met the asphalt. It was hard to say bye, but to make matters worse, I felt terrible that Tom and Yaris had to ride back up the massive mountain for the third time. We took an informal vote and unanimously decided that it would not be cheating to hitchhike up and over the mountain since they had already conquered it, twice. Not two minutes later, we waved down a flatbed trucker who was willing to take them up and over. Luckily it was a quick goodbye. *Thanks for the memories, boys.*

The Rest Of Nevada

My ride through the high deserts of Nevada taught me two things. The more important of the two was that Paul from Germany was right: mountains are the most honest thing in the world. His words kept running through my mind as I experienced new depths to my lactic acid tolerance while riding through the mountains of Nevada. The road seemed to go straight up, topped out at "the pass," and then went straight back down. We followed the black tar path until it went pancake-flat for anywhere from four to forty miles after the bottom of a mountain, then went straight back up the next mountain. It's as if Mother Nature herself said, "I'll give you a break, but you're going to see the next mountain coming toward you the entire time." I had never seen anything like it in my life, but Paul was right; I knew exactly what I was getting into with those mountains. They were brutally honest.

The other lesson learned in Nevada was that I had seriously mismanaged my money situation.

After the first two passes of the day, I was tired, but no more than usual after riding thirty miles. Geoff, on the other hand, was far more enervated than me.

Headed toward our third pass, we hit a false flat that was unusually disheartening. (False flat: a stretch of road that looks to be perfectly flat, but is inexplicably difficult to ride on, usually indicating the road is a one- or two-percent-grade hill.) Combined with a strong headwind and empty stomachs, anyone would break, but to top it off, Geoff had a cable tension problem that was messing up his shifting.

"Get in front of me! I'm just going to sit back here and cuss at nothing," Geoff said.

I got in front and let him draft behind me. Two miles later, I stopped to have lunch.

"These fucking hills and this fucking bike and this fucking wind are pissing me off!" he said, nearly slamming his bike down.

"Yeah?"

"And what are you doing?! Why are we stopping?!"

"It's lunchtime," I said.

"No, it's not! All you want to do is fucking eat!" he yelled.

"What did you say?!" I almost lit straight into him.

"Nothing. Just fucking ignore me. I'm pissed off. These hills are messing with me, and my bike isn't changing gears," Geoff said.

I suggested fixing the cable tension, but he was too upset to think clearly. We kept riding and ate lunch later, stewing in the tension-filled air, while he seemed to slowly cool off. But I was very close to leaving him behind or knocking him out.

That's when I reminded myself that we needed each other to get through this.

I'd started the trip with about $2,000 that I had saved up from working the summer job at camp, and crowd-sourcing funds from friends and family, but after the $1,200 plane ticket, I only had $800 and a dream. Growing up, I had never learned how to be financially responsible, but thinking I could survive on $800 for a trip across the United States was somewhere between brazen and ignorant. There was no way I could have made it without Geoff's help. The least I could do was try to keep both of us motivated and help him cool off a bit when times got tough.

He wasn't the only one who got frustrated, though. It happened mostly in the mornings and evenings, but I would become fiercely depressed. I would shut down and feel a sense of helplessness. The cold had a lot to do with it. Geoff said a few days before Austin that he watched as my mood changed with the setting sun. The cold would affect me physically and mentally, more than it should have, because I had very little cold-weather gear. Nevada kept teaching me lessons, largely at my expense.

That afternoon, it was clear that we needed a good night's sleep. We had every intention of finding a hotel that night and sleeping in warm beds. Of course, that was presuming Ely (pronounced ee-lee) was a town and not just a gas station.

It was odd watching the vehicle coming toward us crest over the next hill. We hadn't seen one in a long time, maybe even the entire day. It was a small white RV with black stripes down the side. The hairs on the back of my neck stood up when they stopped on the other side of the road next to us and asked us if we needed anything. *Uhh... no, I'm good. I don't need any poisoned apples.* We politely declined, insisting we needed to make it to the next town before nightfall, but they said it was over forty miles, and there was no way we would get there on time. Realizing we would be sleeping in the dirt again that night, we chose to hang out with strangers in their RV. *OK. We might as well take it easy then. Poisoned apples it is.*

Steve and Linda were the owners of the RV, and they had completed a family cycle tour a few years back with their kids, who were seven, eleven, and sixteen years old at the time! They'd done a northern route from Washington State to New York, completely self-sustained. It was so great asking them stories about their trip and seeing their eyes light up as they remembered how exciting it had been.

Everyone rode their own bike except the dad, who rode a tandem bike with the seven-year-old. I asked how they felt about their kids being able to endure that kind of riding every day, and they glanced at each other with a look of intense pride. I knew that words couldn't express that kind of feeling. It made me hopeful that my family might have similar memories when I got to be Steve and Linda's age.

After about an hour or so relaxing in their RV, we had to get back to pedaling. We reluctantly left the camper, but they loaded us down with fruit and cookies before we took off, knowing that food is the ultimate way to a cyclist's heart.

Steve and Linda were right, though; there was no way we could have made it to Ely before dark. We were becoming delirious, riding at night with absolutely nothing around. Not a light in sight for miles, except for the truck that had passed us what felt like ages ago.

"I can still see that truck's tail lights," Geoff said.

"You ain't seen't no truck light. You done seen a 'EW-F-O.' I seen't it in a space manual," I said in my deepest southern accent, laughing hysterically, clearly out of my mind. "I heard dem scientists going to send Al Gore up into space to stitch up that ozone layer."

"With whale blubber!" Geoff said, in between laughs.

"But the got dang hippies won't let us shoot da whales!"

We laughed for over an hour, which goes to show

174

that endorphins are one hell of a drug. We were so high on endorphins that sleeping next to a bench in Eureka's city park didn't phase us at all. It was a tolerable place to spend a couple of hours, but we were coming down from our buzz and knew that we wanted to make it to Ely as quickly as possible. We were still nearly forty miles and four thousand feet of climbing away from Ely, but determined to make it the next day.

On the ride from Eureka to Ely, Geoff and I spent a lot of time riding farther apart than normal but always within sight of each other. We weren't necessarily mad, but we just needed time to think while trying to enjoy the day.

Thinking had become a hobby of mine, and I loved being able to zone out into a thought, then come back to reality forty miles down the road. On the second mountain pass between Eureka and Ely, my thinking took me down a path I was not expecting to go down.

Thirteen hundred feet in ten miles. OK, that's not too bad. I can do it. Just put my head down and keep moving. Pull the left pedal up, press the right pedal down, pull the right pedal up, push the left pedal down. Use your glutes. Push through your toes. I can fucking do this, dad. Pull the handlebars. Keep your core tight. Watch me. Go faster. Leave Geoff behind and crush this mountain. Why does he think I won't make it? Quit breathing so sloppy, control it. Slow your heart down. Fuck him. I'm going harder.

I sprinted up the mountain as hard as I could, as fast

as I could, leaning into the pain and proving to myself that I could take it.

I don't need him. Push this fucking bike up this fucking mountain you sack of shit! You can do this. Hell, you are doing this! The finish is just ahead. Sprint!

I drove my legs into the pedals, trying to break the cranks in half. The handlebars warped under my torso as I pulled and pushed on them, hoping to make it to the top of the mountain before my bike or my body broke.

I crested over the top.

I fell over in exhaustion and exploded in tears. Years of pent up anger came pouring out as I came to realization after realization. *Their divorce wasn't my fault. I don't need him to approve of my life. I still love my dad, and I know he still loves me. I'm doing this ride for me, not anyone else.*

I sat and cried uncontrollably.

A few minutes later, after I managed to compose myself, Geoff caught up to me. "What was that?" he asked. "You just hauled ass up that mountain, man."

"Yeah, I know," I said, still trying to control my shaking voice. "I was just working something out."

Ely turned out to be an actual town with a real bed, so we got a good night's sleep, probably too much sleep. It was mid-afternoon when we woke up. With such little daylight left to ride in, we decided to go to the library and update everyone about our trip via social media. While we were there, I also ripped some audiobooks onto my iPod, a little tip that Tom had taught me. Naturally, after a few hours at the library, I was famished, and there was no better place to eat in that town than a Subway in a gas station.

After dinner, we stood outside of the gas station and sipped on our energy drinks. We had decided to have a full night's ride.

"This is such a bad idea," I said, laughing.

"Why? Why is this a bad idea?" Geoff said, getting slightly defensive since it was his idea.

"No. No. I'm all for it; it's just a bad idea. We haven't had a bad idea in a while, so let's do it."

When the failing sun finally went behind the mountain, I put on every bit of cold-weather gear I had: a light jacket, beanie, gloves, and all of my usual "after cycling" clothes. Super caffeinated and excited to mix things up with a night ride, we started pedaling. We tried riding directly out of the small town, but our GPS took us into a trailer park with a gravel road that ended up at a dead end. On our way out of the neighborhood, a pit bull came barreling toward us. My vision focused in, and I couldn't see anything but the gravel in front of us. My pulse was racing so fast it didn't seem cold anymore. Every sense was acutely aware that I was about to get bitten by a dog.

Luckily the pit bull was on the other side of a fence that paralleled the road. When we shined our light on the dog, we could see the pitbull's teeth and the hair on its neck fully raised. *What is it with these dogs, man!?* I wiped the

177

sweat off my forehead, and we kept moving.

About an hour later, Geoff got a flat tire. Again. I laughed at first, attempting to defuse the frustration, but the number of flat tires Geoff got was honestly getting annoying for me. I couldn't imagine how he was feeling. We sat alongside the road on a cliff that overlooked Ely. The mesmerizing lights twinkled in the desert like southern fireflies, sending a twinge of homesickness through me.

As soon as he finished patching the tube, we started climbing the next pass side by side. As we climbed the relentlessly colossal mountain, the dark tortured me. Not knowing how much longer I would have to endure the burning in my legs made every pedal stroke feel like an eternity. I took off my sweat-soaked beanie and jacket to try and cool down. The pitch black mountain pass allowed for no moonlight to help guide us. The full moon, hidden behind the rocks, laughed at me, straining to see the dim light cast on the road from Geoff's bike light. It felt like snails would move up the mountain faster than us.

It was mental torture, but we finally made it to the top after about an hour or so. We could see the next town ahead from the top of the mountain but knew that the desert was a cruel place when it came to distance. Now that we were out of the pass, the lights were crystal clear and seemed to illuminate the entire night sky, but that didn't mean they were close, not by a long shot.

We started bombing down the hill as fast as we

could. Well, as fast as Geoff could, since he was the only one who had a light on his bike. I tried my best to keep us moving quickly, but there wasn't enough light to see all the potholes while riding beside Geoff and I couldn't ride behind him because it was too dark. What happened that night was entirely my fault and a direct result of not having my own bike light, which kept us from moving quickly.

We had to slow to a near crawl because I couldn't navigate the road hazards in the dark, and I didn't want to think about breaking something on my body or bike while in the middle of the desert. We were slamming on the brakes the entire way down the mountain for about an hour, and still hadn't reached the bottom. That was when I noticed the cold really starting to set in.

I went to get a sip of water from my water bottle and heard the ice rattle around inside. *No way, man.* My hands were so numb that I could barely squeeze the brakes, making our descent even more difficult. *I'm so over this shit! This is stupid! Why are we riding at night in the desert?!* I started doing push-ups on my bike while going downhill to get my blood moving faster. Even at such a slow pace, the wind was piercing my clothing straight through to my skin. My sweat became icy. *Suck it up, man. Keep riding.*

I kept my eye on the city lights in the distance, but they were not getting any closer. No matter how much we kept riding, no matter how much I kept pushing through the icy pain in my fingers, no matter what I did to try and warm up, the lights were not getting any closer! *Why not?* I took another sip of my ice water. *This is so stupid.* The words of so many survivalists kept repeating in my head. "Hypothermia can happen in 50 degree weather," they said. I didn't know what the temperature was, but I knew that if the water in my insulated water bottle was freezing, it was effing cold.

I tapped the brakes a bit to slow down. My hands barely moved to touch the levers, but every inch was agonizing. All of my sweat-soaked clothing was now sucking the heat off my body and making it impossible to warm up. *Why aren't the lights getting any closer!?*

That was when I broke.

"I'm fucking done!" I yelled.

I squeezed the brakes as hard as I could, ignoring the icy pain in my fingers. I dismounted my bike and started looking for a place to stop while still rolling. I unclipped my foot from the pedal and started jogging beside the bike. I picked Janice up over my shoulders with the saddlebags dangling off the back rack, and slammed it into the knee-high bushes that covered the ground. I ripped the tent off my bike rack, unrolled it and threw it on the ground, not fifteen feet from the road.

"Where's my clothes?!" I said, throwing everything out of my pack to find something dry and warm to wear. "Geoff set the tent up! I'm done bro!"

"Yeah, I'm working on it," he said, calmly laying his

bike down.

The spot I'd chosen to set up the tent was about three feet smaller in both directions than the tent's size, but it was the biggest clearing around. The entire area, for as far as our lights would let us see, was covered in sharp, round shrubs that kept scratching my legs. The area was so small that we couldn't put the tent stakes in and had to rely on pole tension to keep the tent up. I didn't care.

Realizing I had nothing dry or warm to wear, I took off all my icy, wet clothes and got in my sleeping bag naked. I buried myself in my bag and immediately felt a rock under my shoulder. I pressed into it harder, to make sure I could still feel something. I don't remember falling asleep that night; I just passed out.

The next morning there was a weird tension between Geoff and me. Nothing negative, but just tense. He had never seen me, or probably anyone else, have a mental breakdown like that. As soon as I put pants on, which were cracking from the frozen sweat, I apologized for freaking out the night before and promised never to complain about being cold again. Nothing in my life had ever pushed me to such a point, and being that cold was, without a doubt, one of the most uncomfortable moments in my life. The cold had finally broken me mentally and emotionally. It was a surreal low for me and one that I will never forget. It was Nevada's last lesson to me before Utah.

Utah

Dear Lord, please do not let Utah be like Nevada. As the saying goes: ask, and it might happen, or something like that. There was a little hotel appropriately named The Border Inn at the border between Nevada and Utah, where we got some wildly mediocre food that tasted like manna from heaven. After being out in the desert for so long, eating a hamburger and fries in a hopeless, run-down casino was the dream, and we were living it. We didn't want to risk catching whatever bugs were crawling around in the grungy hotel, so we decided to sleep outside, about four hundred yards away from the inn, on public land. We could see Utah in the distance and knew that we had survived the loneliest road in America. We'd summited seventeen mountain passes, climbed 20,062 feet, and covered 378 miles throughout the state. *Utah, please don't be like Nevada!*

It was our last night in the lonely state, and if we pedaled fast enough the next few days, we could meet back up with Ashley, our friend who'd helped get us started back in Seattle. She was in St. George, Utah, for a conference, and we were just a few hundred miles away. We decided to take a slight detour south and meet her.

It took us two more nights of stealth camping before we hit Interstate 15, and what a wild ride that was. We topped out at an insane fifty miles per hour on the interstate, and managed to average thirty-eight miles per hour for nearly forty miles, coming down the back side of the mountain. And all the while, we were dodging debris and potholes, ignoring the whizzing traffic, and continuously looking over our shoulders as we crossed over the exit ramps. Taking the interstate had been a shifty move, but we covered over one hundred miles in less than a day and had plenty of energy left to hang out with Ashley. *Sketchy yet satisfying.*

I was so happy to find that Ashley was perfectly content just chilling in the hotel with two absolutely disheveled guys. The most exciting thing we did was go out to eat, where we realized there was no alcohol sold in Utah on Sundays. To remedy that gargantuan problem, Ashley drove us to Arizona. Once back at the hotel, we dumped piles of candy in the center of a king-sized bed, watched *American Dad*, and had a couple of beers. Our stay with Ashley could not have been better.

It was a short visit, but seeing a familiar face made a world of difference when all Geoff and I had to look at were each other's bedraggled selves. After a quick goodbye, we were off to ride to Zion National Park, but it didn't take long before I needed food.

I sat across from Geoff in silence, shoveling McDonalds hash browns into my mouth with no regard for my appearance or manners. I showered the night before, but one shower was not enough to get all the dirt off me from biking the loneliest road. I had layers of grime on me that radiated enough stink to fill an entire arena. Even if we had access to it, a shower with cheap hotel soap couldn't possibly bring me up to society's hygiene standard. However, my stench didn't stop a woman in her late fifties from coming up and talking to us.

She approached our booth and got uncomfortably close. Her thighs almost touched the edge of our table. She asked why we were dressed in spandex, and why we were riding bicycles. As I told her about our trip, tears welled up in her eyes. I became intensely uneasy. Had I said something to offend her? I quit droning on about why we were riding and paused to let her speak.

"You need to be careful riding. It's dangerous out there." One of her tears rolled down her face. "Accidents happen, and drivers can kill a cyclist easily, so be sure to stay safe," she said as another tear dropped to the floor. She left without saying anything else.

I know there was a story there. Maybe it was her driving. Maybe it was her child who was hit. "Maybe" is all she left me with. I hope she can muster up the courage to tell her story one day, so we can all learn from it.

The woman's words stuck with me as we rode that day.

We managed to get about forty miles in and decided to stealth camp near Zion at a place called Coal Pits Wash, to spend the next day exploring the park. It turned out, a lot of people had the same idea, and we ended up camping with about forty strangers on the side of the road. We never knew what to expect when we got to a destination, but riding up to that many people pulled over on the side of the road was an odd experience. It felt like they were well manicured vagabonds like ourselves. After laying down the tarp, putting the sleeping pads on it, and rolling out the sleeping bags (no need for the tent anymore; we were weathered enough), we did some mild exploring. I didn't realize it at first, but Coal Pits Wash was actually just outside the park, explaining why so many people chose to camp here. *Free is better than paying to sleep in the dirt.*

Was it a good thing that we were willing to stay with a camp full of traveling trespassers? After all, camping there was not entirely legal. But it was just as likely they were asking the same question about us. We were all just nature enthusiasts looking to get an early start at sunrise.

The next morning, I woke with an icy pain shooting through my feet and fingertips, but kept that bit of information to myself, having promised Geoff I wouldn't mention the cold anymore. But I couldn't hide that I was refusing to get out of my sleeping bag. Waking up on that particularly chilly morning took much longer than it should have, and I could tell Geoff was getting annoyed by the way he was packing up to leave and staying relatively silent. I took so long to mentally wake up, that by the time I managed to unzip my cocoon, over half of the other campers had left. *Well, at least we're not the last ones to leave.*

I slowly packed up my sleeping bag, rolled my sleep pad up, and zipped up my panniers. The sound of people laughing and car doors shutting told me that everyone was excited to head towards the park. I straddled my bike to set off toward the park as well. I took a brief look at the once bustling campsite and saw only dirt. *Geez. I know I'm slow, but everyone else must have also been really fast. Well, at least we don't have to say bye to anyone.*

Our map told us the road into Zion National Park was steep and winding. A couple of miles after breakfast, we rode up a fairly steep and winding road, reaching the top and thinking the tough part was over. *That wasn't so bad.*

We began seeing signs for Rockville shortly after that. Maybe I should not have been surprised that a town called Rockville had shops that sold geodes and gems. My inner child was thrilled. I have always loved gemstones and rock mining. Other than the occasional gem shack, the town was nothing but cows and horses. The sign we passed said, "Pop. 247." I saw three people while riding through, and one of them was an infant. At three people strong, this was still not the most deserted town we had seen, which kept blowing my mind.

After Rockville, we went through one of the best outdoorsman tourist traps in the world: Springdale, Utah. In the town, nestled right at the south entrance to Zion, everyone carried a water bottle or wore a CamelBak. They all sported top-of-the-line hiking shoes and had aggressively shredded calf muscles. This was hiking country, and I felt fiercely out of place. However, the locals were friendly, and the tourists were all just as lost and in amazement as I was. I'm not sure why I didn't associate myself with the tourists, because I was exactly like them, only on a bicycle. But somehow we seemed different; not better, just different.

After Springdale, we entered the park. Zion was easily one of the most beautiful places I had ever visited. The pink and yellow rock walls, the crystal clear streams, and the fairy-tale wildlife all made it breathtakingly gorgeous. We stopped near the outer edges of the camping area, leaned our bikes against a tree, and locked our bikes together, hoping that would be enough to deter any opportunistic thief. We never liked to lock our bikes up on trees in national parks, because of the rules against harming the flora and fauna.

Geoff had the great idea of filming our hike so we could show everyone back home how beautiful it was, but the camera died after filming for thirty seconds, just before we started hiking into the Emerald Pools.

After our hike, we returned to our bikes and headed east through the park. As I rode through the canyons, weaving alongside the river, I had to constantly slow down to dodge the other tourists. There were so many people on the sidewalk paths that people were forced to walk on the street. The people were cluttering the natural beauty of the area. I couldn't help but feel a bit irritated.

While dealing with the frustrating human obstacles, I was also remembering that Geoff wanted to leave Utah to make it to the Grand Canyon on his birthday. But this tour around Zion was eating a ton of time. *We can't do all of these trails, ride along the entire park, and expect to make it to the Grand Canyon on time.* We had gotten much better at putting up with each other's habits, but his attitude and undue pressure to get moving was chipping away at my understanding. He was becoming more irate, and my tolerance for him was coming to an end. He was mad about the goals he himself had set, knowing full well that we couldn't accomplish all of them.

Regardless of my increasing frustration toward Geoff, the only bad part about the actual park was the "goat heads," as we learned to call them. These things wreaked havoc on our tires. Goat heads are thorny burrs that look like a bull's skull, with the thorns being the bull's horns, protruding out, waiting to stab something. Geoff was unfortunate enough to continually find them in his tires. Pulling the trailer only made it worse since he had four tires to keep patching, instead of just two. It's one reason I will never tour with a trailer again.

As it turned out, we'd read the map wrong. The map description that warned us about the hill into Zion actually read, "the road ascending to the tunnel in Zion is steep and winding." The map was right. Brutally right. We were now on that road. Each section was only a hundred yards or so, but each section of the switchback seemed to get steeper. I laughed at how vertical the road was. I could have stood straight up on that hill, reached my arm out, and touched the asphalt in front of me. The gentleman at the top of the road, guarding the tunnel entrance, shouted down, "Why don't you just walk? It might be faster." *Good question, my man. It's either pride or stubbornness. I'll let you know when I figure it out.*

The narrow road was impressive, though. It had weaved through a canyon first and now dipped into the tunnel entrance in the giant rock face, allowing traffic to flow only one direction at a time. It was physically impossible for a vehicle and bicycle to coexist in such a narrow tunnel, so we had to exercise our thumbs and grab a ride on the back of a flatbed truck. Luckily we had chosen to play it safe because the only lights in the tunnel were from the dim, flickering bulbs that were spaced out every 20 yards or so. I shut my eyes to take a quick nap on the bed of the truck; ten minutes later, we were through. Geoff and I couldn't live with the guilt of not having officially ridden the entire length of America, so we vowed to ride the tunnel's distance, an additional 1.1 miles, after we finished the tour, to make up for it.

We thanked the gentleman for giving us a ride and rode a little while longer, until we exited the park and found a place beside the road with an awe-inspiring view near Mt. Carmel Junction. The edge of the road dropped straight down ten feet and then leveled back out just enough for the both of us to roll out a tarp and lie down. It was great finding such accessible places to sleep, but it was a comically long night. I had to listen to an animal wrestle around in the bushes, no more than a foot from my bed, all night. The morning brought with it a gentle fog that slowly burned away as the golden sunrise reflected off the white sand of the canyons. *Zion National Park would be jealous.* It was by far the best way to say goodbye to Utah.

Arizona

Zion was beautiful, and the white sandy canyons at Mt. Carmel Junction showed me a matchless sunrise, but that tourist attraction had thrown a wrench in Geoff's plan to make it to the Grand Canyon on his birthday. We were still 223 miles from our destination, with only two days to get there. In a perfect world where we had a tailwind, no goat heads, no Buckskin Mountain range in the way, and enough calories to fuel two cycling human garbage disposals, 223 miles was doable. But that wasn't the case. We were forever stopping to change flat tires, and struggling between sightseeing and cycling, and we still couldn't seem to ever fully recover, both physically and mentally. Not to mention, getting to the Grand Canyon on a specific day was Geoff's plan and not mine. I'm all about pushing myself, but

Arizona

I tend to get a bit hostile when I'm not the one pushing. Geoff had been my best friend for over nine years, but there was a tension building between us, eroding away any foundation our friendship had built.

On the first day into Arizona, we made it forty-five miles, with only 1,700 feet of elevation gain and 3,635 feet of elevation loss. It was a perfect morning, and I loved the downhill, but even when the cycling gods looked down on us, and everything went right, I was still becoming increasingly tired of riding. I mean, completely done with it. The thrill of adventure had become the drudgery of a day's job, a state all endurance adventurists face, I'm sure. On top of the monotony of it all, Geoff kept pressing his thumb in the wound by setting unnecessary deadlines. *I want to go home. At what point is continuing still worth it? What else do I have to gain from this trip?*

Nightfall was closing in on us, and the lovely morning had turned into a cold, wet evening. The slight rain started to soak through my clothes and with it, the same bone-chilling cold that had overtaken me in Nevada. Geoff was on edge about every comment I made on the weather or any state of discomfort we were in, so I kept my mouth shut. I kept riding, pushing myself up steeper and steeper hills. Not only had the weather turned, but the uphill climbs had returned. Sweating harder and getting colder, I kept riding to try and get as far as possible. But as we climbed uphill on Route 89A, lightning struck under the massive thunderheads creeping toward us.

"Geoff, we need to find a place to camp. The rain is about to get a lot worse."

"Come on, man!" he replied. "Let's make it to Jacobs Lake before we camp!"

Jacobs Lake was another twenty miles, and from the looks of the terrain we were riding, all uphill.

"Dude, what does it matter?" I said, knowing it would piss him off. "We can make it up tomorrow! We can't change the weather."

There was no reply. Just silence as we pedaled up and down the hills. I pulled in front of him once it flattened out a bit and said, "Let's stop here. There's a flat spot to pitch the tent. I'm not riding anymore today."

"Are you serious?!" he said, hesitantly hitting the brakes and coming to a stop, "It's just rain, when did that ever hurt you?" He leaned his bike up against a tree.

"I'm not kidding, man, I'm done riding today. We can make it up tomorrow!" My frustration turned to anger as I wrestled with untying my sleeping bag.

"No, we won't. You'll get tired or cold or something and come up with another excuse to stop! You're the reason we won't make it to the Grand Canyon on time!"

"Shut up, dude. Just go to sleep," I said

"Don't tell me to shut up!" He started walking closer.

We're about to fight. Geoff has never fought in his life. WTF?

Arizona

He reached the trailer between the two of us and pulled his tent out. "Have fun sleeping in the rain," he said.

The passive-aggressive fight building between us had finally come to a head in the middle of an Arizona rainstorm. I didn't mind sleeping outside the tent since I could barely stand to look at Geoff, much less sleep inches away from him. I leaned my bike up next to the thickest pine tree I could find and laid my sleep pad and sleeping bag on the ground under it. To keep the rain off, I tucked one side of the blue tarp between the bike and the tree, then wrapped the tarp over and around my bike, and tucked the other side under my sleep pad, creating a two-second lean-to shelter. It kept the rain off, but the wind whipped the loud, crinkling tarp back and forth all night, often smacking me in the face. I slept like a screaming baby. *I want to go home.*

The morning after came slowly and with heavy fog. I'd hardly slept, so waking was a reprieve from the torturous tarp, and I looked forward to it. I did not look forward to hashing things out with Geoff.

I made instant mix coffee that steeped slowly in the tension-filled air. It was Geoff's birthday, and we were still 178 miles from the south entrance to Grand Canyon National Park. Guilt wracked and anxious, I sat and watched an ant crawl around the coffee pot. I had let Geoff down. I was part of the reason we hadn't made it on time; somewhere deep in my gut, I knew I could have pushed harder.

Geoff got out of his tent just as the coffee finished

and slowly sauntered over. I poured Geoff's coffee into his travel mug and handed it to him. I finished the coffee pot off and we sat across from each other, waiting for the other to speak first. The hot caffeine rush allowed my mouth to start sputtering out a garbled mess of words, in an attempt to apologize.

I told him I was stressing about money, and that I was truly tired of the monotony of the trip. Geoff talked about how he was having a quarter-life crisis. It was his twenty-fifth birthday. This adventure was supposed to be when he would learn about himself and the direction he wanted life to go, but the epiphanies were not coming to him.

"That's why I was agitated," he said, "and I know it was an unrealistic goal that didn't matter, but once I set a goal, I want to achieve it. I know I was pushing you too much for my own pride. That's my bad."

We eventually came up with two rules:

1. Respect each other
2. Say what you mean

After that, we never argued again.

We had not realized it the night before, but the flat spot where we'd chosen to sleep was actually a gravel drive-way. I laughed at the thought of someone pulling away from their house to find me sleeping under my bicycle. We rode away from our temporary home in silence, reflecting on the trip so far and how we would go about completing it. After a while, the silent reflection became a bit overwhelming, so I put in my earbuds and listened to the *Harry Potter and the Sorcerer's Stone* audiobook. I'd never thought listening to an audiobook would be very entertaining while working out, but I'm glad I was wrong. It was more than entertainment, though. I needed something to remove my mind from everything so I could process the day's events. Listening to the book gave me a break from reality and a chance to reset.

Arizona is exceptionally scenic and beautiful, but I've never really cared for awe-inspiring scenery. If I've seen it on TV or a magazine, then I've seen it already. Sometimes a sunrise or landscape feature will strike me, but I'm more entertained by what I'm doing at the moment, and right then, it was cycling.

We were riding through the Buckskin Mountain range when the voice of Harry Potter said, "I found it, something I was finally great at."

Pedaling along that dusty cliffside, with not a cloud in the sky, I started to cry. I hung my head as tears dropped onto my sunglasses. I have always wanted to be great at something, but my blessed curse is to be a "jack of all trades, master of none." Hearing those words made me realize I was in the middle of finding my greatness. Maybe it's everyone's desire to be great at something, but it's ingrained deep in me. Hearing Harry find his call to greatness made me aware that my answer was closer than I had thought. I was currently, actively engaged in my own self-development and becoming who I wanted to be.

I rode with a real intensity that day until we reached a little hotel called Cliff Dwellers Lodge and decided to take a break from sleeping on the ground. We walked in, and while Geoff was picking up some celebratory brews from one of the hotel clerks, I told the other guys behind the counter that it was his birthday. They seemed honored that two disheveled cyclists would choose to celebrate in their hotel, so they let us play pool for free all night. It doesn't seem like much, but it meant the world to us. We needed to relax, and it was perfect.

We may have celebrated Geoff's birthday a bit too much because we woke up just before noon and begrudgingly got on our bikes.

A history lesson from the guys at the lodge helped us make sense of the massive, carved-out boulders that we passed later in the day. A Native American tribe had lived there and carved out cave dwellings in the side of the cliffs. We briefly stopped to check out the former houses.

The previous night's soiree and the unexpected history detour must have satiated our spirits and legs, because we made it eighty-one miles to Cameron, Arizona, where we camped alongside the road in an RV park that offered little to no coziness. The middle of the desert is a perfect place to feel as small and exposed as possible, and this RV park did a great job of exacerbating those feelings. We didn't spend much time there because I still felt terrible for not making it to the Grand Canyon on time, not to mention that I knew making it to the canyon would mean a break from riding.

We woke up early the next morning and made a bee-line straight for Grand Canyon National Park, but despite all our efforts, the cycling gods demanded that we slow down our journey. Geoff got a flat tire around thirty miles into the day, so we fixed it and kept going. A few miles later, he got another flat and became so frustrated that he suggested we stop for the day. *I mean... I'm done if you're done.*

We slept on the roadside without pitching our tent again, just another night sleeping in a dew-soaked bag, hoping not to get eaten.

The next morning, we woke up full of energy and ready to ride. We knew we were close to the canyon and that we'd reach it today, no matter what happened. Just a few miles in, we passed the sign announcing that we had entered the park. Suddenly the whole landscape changed. The trees became lush and tall. There was shrubbery everywhere that pressed right up to the edge of the road. The rolling hills made for a nice change of pace, and we loved every second of the newness.

Around thirty miles later, we reached the campground, but instead decided to get a hotel room. Geoff wanted to enjoy his time at the park, and I was just along for the ride. I must say, though, hanging out in that hotel room, eating junk food and watching *King of the Hill*, was one of the most memorable nights of the trip for no other reason than a sense of accomplishment. We had battled the weather, the roads, and each other to make it to that point, but we had made it. We were pushing our limits to find out who we really were, and the cost had nearly broken us, but everything was as it should be for that night. It was time to relax and enjoy the moment because what lay ahead would push those boundaries again, and we needed to be ready for it.

Quitters Always Say Die

After a much-needed recovery night, we took all the bags and gear off our bikes and rode a few miles to the canyon. Riding a bike that's forty pounds lighter makes all the difference in the world. It felt like we were Olympic-level fast with little to no effort. It made those few miles of familiar evergreen trees, winding roads, and scenic wildlife some of my favorites of the entire trip.

After we got off our bikes and locked them up, we walked toward the canyon and started our day's adventure with the incredible view of the giant hole in the ground. It is an awe-inspiring sight to see something that almost looks photoshopped, but can kill someone if they take a wrong step. Remembering that my great-uncle had blacked out about fifty feet down into the canyon, ultimately drowning in water only a few inches deep, I had a healthy respect for the area. It felt as though I could reach out and touch the other side of the canyon. *Put your hand down, you idiot.* I could have stayed at the rim for hours, but as usual, we were on a timeline and couldn't spend all day there. The hike down into the canyon was a bit crowded, but I didn't mind. The tourists gave us plenty of room to walk, probably because I looked so unkempt that they didn't want to be any closer than necessary, so it worked out in our favor.

The trail was packed down hard from thousands of people walking over it every year. In front of us, fellow trail goers shuffled their feet, kicking the fine sand and creating a dust cloud, given the lack of rain. The silty air worked its way deep into my beard and lungs. *I will never be clean again. It doesn't matter what I do; I will always have dirt and sweat on me... forever.*

After we'd walked downhill for as long as we could stand it, I looked back and realized that we were still very much at the top of the canyon. There was no way I would walk to the Colorado River, make it back up this cliff, and still be willing to ride the next day. I honestly had no idea of the vastness of that place. We could have stayed there a week and not scratched the surface of what it had to offer. Hiking out of the canyon was tough, but realizing we had no time to experience its greatness was a much bigger pill to swallow. *I'll be back, you big-ass hole, I'll be back.*

The next morning, we left the park and started heading south again. The average temperature at the Grand Canyon during late October is around mid 70's during the day and low 30's at night. Normally, that would be perfect riding weather, but while we were there, it was a bit below average and getting colder. Also, I still didn't have any proper cold-weather gear. Riding in the morning and at night was becoming increasingly difficult because of the dew and the temperature dipping, so we planned to keep heading south, like migrating birds in hopes of dodging the weather.

We arrived in Williams, Arizona, just in time for the post office to lock their doors. I had never wanted a package so intensely in my life. Kaitlyn had mailed my box of cold-weather gear a week ago, and I knew it had arrived. My initial plan was for Kaitlyn to ship the clothes to San Francisco, but while it was chilly, it wasn't unbearably cold and I didn't want to carry all the extra clothes. Then, I planned on her shipping it to the next place we stopped for more than a few days, but we never stayed anywhere long enough. I finally decided for her to ship it to a town that I would be nearby in a week. Williams, Arizona, was that town and I arrived at the post office at 6:15 PM. The thought of all my warm jackets, proper thermal pants, and winter Under Armour shirts sitting behind those locked post office doors gnawed at my brain like a parasite. I could have been warm that night, but instead, I would go to bed cold. Again. I was about to cry when Geoff said, "It's going to be twenty-one degrees tonight." *I had better not cry... I need to save the water in my body so I can pee on myself to warm up tonight.*

Of course, I never actually peed on myself, but I'm not above it. I would do anything to stay warm. Geoff was also not imagining a good night's sleep in the woods, especially after our luxurious stay on actual mattresses the nights before. But we both agreed, we had to get back to the tour. We wanted to tour a certain way: sleeping in the dirt, cheap and relaxed. We had started to lose focus of those goals, so we decided to stealth camp across the street from a Denny's, but not before dining in, dusty and desultory. While sitting in the booth, enjoying the last bit of heat for the night, I used Geoff's iPad and forwarded my cold-weather gear to Flagstaff so we didn't have to wait around for the post office to open in the morning.

After dinner, we walked across the street and rolled our bikes into the woods far enough that no one could see us. We set up the tent and went to sleep. I was already jackhammering from the cold, but my sleeping bag always managed to warm me up enough just before I fell asleep. I wasn't sure if it was twenty minutes or four hours later, but I woke up to flashing blue lights and Geoff getting out of the tent. *Hurry up and give us the fine. Better yet, take me to jail so I can get warmed up. I just want to go back to sleep.*

Not caring about what was happening, at all, I listened as Geoff explained to the cops that we were staying here for the night, and we would be gone before the sun

205

came up.

"OK," he said. "I'll be back here at zero six hundred. I don't want to see you, gentlemen, anywhere near here." As quickly as they had shown up, they were gone, and I fell back asleep before Geoff was even in the tent. *Woken up by the cops; that's a new one for me.*

We left the "campsite" at the crack of dawn and spent another day in Williams to kill time, since it was now Sunday and the post office was closed anyways. We rode around, looking for a sunny park to loiter in and once we found it, sat in the sun all day. Uneventful, sure, but to a cycle tourist, these days are some of the most impactful. It's a moment to reflect, enjoy the day, not exercise, and appreciate the experience. *I think I'm done riding.*

Geoff offered to get a hotel room so we didn't meet the cops in the middle of the night, again. I was good with it. I needed to call Kaitlyn.

When I was in high school, I remember learning that one of the most dangerous times for a person in a survival situation is during the rescue. After days, weeks, or months with minimal food, possible sustained injuries, and dangerously low vitals, the relief of seeing the rescue team allows the survivor to turn over control of their situation mentally. They end up relaxing too much, and the stress that had been keeping them alive goes away. The last moments of their life are spent watching the rescue team come to try and save them.

Granted, I physically survived the trip and was never in any perilous survival situation. Still, all of the time spent relaxing at the canyon had made me not want to ride anymore, and I truly felt like my time riding had come to an end. I had a taste of comfort, and I was handing in my will to keep going. We had ridden a couple of thousand miles, seen more of the country than most people ever would, and met some fantastic people along the way. Still, I also battled with self-deprecating thoughts of failure, knowing that even my dad didn't think I would finish the trip, and to top it off, Geoff had had to fund the whole thing. I was convincing myself that my dad was right: I was a bum with self-aggrandizing visions of fulfilling some higher destiny, but in the end, I was just coasting through life. It was time for me to go home and start figuring out how to be a better person.

That night, I called Kaitlyn and told her that I wanted to come home. I said I was going to fly back to South Carolina and start working to pay back Geoff. I confessed with tears streaming down my face that I was tired of relying on people to get me through life. I had started this trip to do something great, but all I had done was strain the relationship between Geoff and me. My body hurt around the clock, and I was tired of the fucking cold! Not to mention, I was so incredibly annoyed about having to fake a smile every time someone asked where I was going. I just wanted to be left alone, and Geoff felt the same way.

Kaitlyn sympathized with me for a while. Then she

said, "Imagine how you would feel if you quit now. You would beat yourself up for the rest of your life." She knew the exact twenty words to say to make me shut the hell up and keep pushing forward. It felt good knowing that she would selflessly push me toward my goals even though I was broken and wanting to quit. Certainly a quality that none of my past girlfriends had possessed. That was the kind of woman I needed in my life, and I had found her.

I woke up to the smell of stale coffee, stained carpet, and presumably clean sheets in a run-down hotel. It had been a long night, full of rejuvenating hope and excitement. That morning, I joyfully got on my bike and we rode on to Flagstaff, where we stayed with some folks we had met on-line and who had done quite a bit of adventuring themselves. They were around our age, knew exactly where the good food in town was, and wanted to hang out, drink beers, and swap stories. It was refreshing to meet people who gave us our personal space, yet still wanted to hang out.

Riding through the desert had made me feel so isolated and ready to quit, but I had lost sight of the main reason I wanted to ride across America: to see America itself. Sure this country has beautiful landscapes, but that's not what makes it worth seeing; it's the people that make this country what it is, and that's what I had forgotten. In Flagstaff, I started to reprioritize what I thought was important about this journey.

Flagstaff signified a fundamental turning point in my

attitude, not only because I found a renewed sense of purpose for the trip, but because it was where I finally got my cold-weather gear. I was so happy to put on my long-sleeve Under Armour shirt, wind- and waterproof cycling jacket, and two pairs of long thermal pants. I was finally warm, and that made all the difference in my outlook toward riding. Flagstaff was where I started having fun again.

After a brief tour around Flagstaff, we made our way to Sedona. An easy forty miles with a 4,200-foot drop in elevation made for an incredibly relaxing day of riding. The only down side was the sun beaming straight into my retinas. As much as it sucked, I was thankful I couldn't see all the trash we were riding over. The sun's reflection bouncing off all the shattered glass scattered on the road looked like miles of twinkling stars. *Please don't pop a tire... please.*

Once we got to Red Rock State Park in Sedona, Geoff was again enamored with the thought of hiking, while I was elated to do anything but ride for the day. We went on a short hike through the park to a waterfall but couldn't stay long because we needed to make it another twenty miles to Cornville, before nightfall. We had made a reservation with a Warmshowers.org host weeks prior.

We kept our promise to stay the night. Of course, we showed up late to the house, because that's how cycle-touring goes, but our host didn't seem to mind. We got in, and he showed us to our separate bedrooms. *Separate rooms!? I haven't slept by myself in over a month. The cycle-tour gods are good!* We washed up and walked out into the living room, where our host was cooking us spaghetti that was so good it made my tongue slap my brain. We spent the night swapping tour stories, and his made cycling across America feel like taking a stroll in a park.

After a relaxing night, we woke up ready to ride toward Prescott. While packing our clothes onto our bikes in the garage, I looked up and saw nearly twenty race bibs clipped together and hanging from the wall. I do the same thing with my bibs, but many of his were full Ironman Triathlon bibs, a much more difficult race than any I had ever run. Another set of bibs I had never seen before, that had "ITI350" and "ITI1000" on them. These bibs were separate from the Ironman bibs, like they were altogether different. Like the Ironman bibs were unworthy to touch them. When our host walked out, I had to ask him what race that was, and with a slight grin, he said, "Oh, have you heard of the Iditarod?"

"Of course," I said. I knew all about it because my favorite author, Gary Paulsen, known for writing *Hatchet*, loved the Iditarod and often referenced the famous dog race in his books.

"Well," he said, "this is a run, walk, or bike race that follows the dog race's same path. It usually starts a few days after the Iditarod."

My jaw slammed into the ground. This guy was a genuine badass. I knew it was cold during the Iditarod, but our host began telling us about the negative-fifty-degree race with its gale-force winds and waist-deep snow. I was having a hard time being sweat covered in twenty-one degree weather, but this guy's suffering made me ashamed to have ever complained about the cold. He was humble about the race and had competed in it with the sole purpose of pushing himself as hard as he could.

In the brief time we spent in that garage, I realized that I should stop complaining so much about the discomforts of the trip because I was willingly putting myself through it. I had dreamed of this trip for years, and now here I was, grumbling through it. I've always needed a little perspective to readjust my outlook on life, and this man, who had lived in the desert his entire life, then competed in the coldest thousand-mile race on the planet, had just given it to me. It was time to start riding again, but now I was reinvigorated and ready for what was to come.

"Have fun on the ride to Jerome," he said with a devilish smile. "It can get a bit hilly." *Awesome. If he thinks it's hilly, then it's got to be a mountain.*

We covered 1,526 feet of elevation in five miles. It was no light effort to make it to Jerome, but the nifty historical site was worth it, even though it wasn't quite the "ghost town" they advertised it to be. The quaint shops and scenic overlooks made me want to stop and see what it had to offer. But our detours had taken up a lot of time over the past weeks, and I wanted to use this newfound motivation, so we pedaled past the town. We covered about fifty miles that day with a 5,000-foot elevation gain and a 2,800-foot elevation loss. It was a challenging ride, and as the day came to a close, we were in the middle of Yavapai Hills.

Sleeping on mattresses for the past few days had made us soft, which made our decision to sleep in the dirt difficult. But the idea of sleeping in the middle of the city made us both a bit uncomfortable, not to mention it was Halloween night and everyone would be out late.

As we rode past a big box home improvement store, I noticed that the tool sheds in the parking lot were open. *We've slept in worse spots than that for sure.* I somehow convinced Geoff that we should stay the night in one of them and leave super early, before any employees showed up to work. He was hesitant at first but realized it was better than sleeping behind a strip mall, or underneath a bridge.

As we sat outside of a Dollar General, watching the employees leave the home improvement store, it felt appropriate to be eating candy and chugging sodas on Halloween. It seemed like we sat there for hours, waiting until we could sneak into the sheds, but the wait was well worth it. "Welcome back, old friend," I said as I slid into my sleeping bag. It felt good to be touring our way again. I spent the night vibrating from sugar and caffeine, but when I finally came down from my sugar buzz, it was the best sleep I had gotten in weeks.

Right before I fell asleep, I thought about how I

would have missed nights like this if I had quit. I would have missed out on that incredible spaghetti. I would never have learned that people run the Iditarod course after the dog race. I would have missed everything the rest of America had to offer. I shut my eyes and slept like a baby.

What felt like moments later, Geoff's alarm went off and my eyes slammed open. We'd set the alarm to go off one hour before the home improvement store opened, hoping to miss the employees coming in. I cracked the door to the shed and saw at least three employees already in the store, and two more walking to the door. *Well, the early bird catches the trespassing cycle tourists, I suppose.* We quickly and quietly packed our gear and waited for everyone to go inside. As the door closed behind them, we practically fell out of the shed with our bikes, unintentionally making as much noise as possible. *Smooth. Real smooth.* We hastily got on our bikes and rode away, acting as natural as a barrel full of fish at a gun store. *I'm cool—nothing to see here. Move along.*

It was 126 miles to get to Phoenix. Since we had no intention of riding on the interstate again, especially for a hundred miles, we opted instead to go the long way around, through Yarnell. Luckily, it was nearly all downhill and easily the most relaxing ride of the trip. We rode through the arid Arizona landscape with ease, traversing all 126 miles with around 3,100 feet of elevation gain and a massive 7,500 feet of elevation loss. The majority of it went something like this: pedal, pedal, coast... pedal, pedal, coast.... The sun, and more importantly, the wind, was at our backs, and we had plenty of peanut butter and jelly tortilla sandwiches to fuel our day's ride. Life couldn't have been any better. But then we got to Phoenix.

Phoenix was the most annoying place to ride a bicycle. It was full of traffic and built in the most mundane traffic grid I'd ever seen. We played leapfrog with a bus for miles as we hit stoplight after stoplight. The exhaust from the cars was bad, but I will never forget the way the thick black smoke from that bus took my lungs hostage. I struggled to breath every time that bus passed us. The city was plain and flat, with only fast food chains and corporate buildings to look at. I was bored out of my mind until we found the Arizona Canal Trail. This little slice of heaven got us off the main roads, but it wasn't visually appealing. Most of the trail was packed gravel with some graffitied, paved sections; it seemed like a trail perfectly designed to fit into a Tony Hawk video game. The human-made canal probably carried the city's runoff water out to a river heading to the sea. The bike path extended out between eight and twenty feet on either side of it. It wasn't the best or the worst, but I was thankful for the twenty miles we rode on it. Every city needs some way for people to get from end to end without having to battle with traffic, and for that, Phoenix, I thank you.

After a night in Phoenix, we made it to Superior,

Arizona, where we kept our previously made Warmshowers reservation and stayed with a host who had created a haven for cycle tourists to relax. They had an Airstream outside their house and allowed people to stay as long as they wanted, for free. Since we had ridden hard the past couple of days, we couldn't pass up the offer. Not to mention, our host had a massive movie collection, which is my key to decompression.

Our host was a jolly guy with a big laugh and a sense of adventure and I liked him immediately. His gigantic dog, a male Newfoundland, weighing in at 150 pounds, didn't hurt his case either. These folks were genuine and sincere people who went out of their way to serve cycle tourists, and I could not thank them enough. As he took us outside to the Airstream, I looked around in amazement at his landscaping decor. There were empty flower pots, random stone statues, and some colorful glass art scattered about the property. But I was gobsmacked when I noticed he had forty-one chairs in his yard, which made me laugh at first. But then my mind wandered off as to why he had so many. *Does this guy host huge parties? Does he like to sit in multiple places to get a different perspective of his yard? Does he own a chair business? Is he using the chairs to poke holes in his lawn for aeration?*

That night, I lay down intending to fall into the deepest of sleep, but my gut had other intentions. Without going into details, I got sick two or three times. So, our plan to stay there one night ended up turning into three nights, since it took a while for me to rehydrate enough to pedal through the desert.

While we were there, I decided to do a statistical recap of our trip so far.

Geoff's Stats:
- Six flat tires on the bike and fourteen on the trailer
- Five wrecks (three sand wipeouts, one train track wreck, and one stoplight fall)

Shaun's Stats:
- Five flat tires on the bike
- Two wrecks (overcompensated at Grand Canyon and a wreck in Wimberly)
- Hit in the face seven times (four yellow jackets, two beetles, and one enormous locust that scared the shit out of me)

All in all, the rest from the night of being sick was great, but I was eager to get back to riding. We hit the road that morning intending to go as far as we could, which ended up being 102 miles, to the other side of a mountain in Safford, Arizona. It was the last night we would spend in Arizona.

New Mexico

The day after Safford was another ninety-eight miles to Lordsburg, New Mexico, followed by a ninety-mile day to Columbus, just on Mexico's border. To get to Columbus, we took New Mexico Route 9, which paralleled the Mexican border for miles, with nothing in sight except the occasional border patrol vehicle. We had a forty-mile stretch with no water and nowhere to fill up, so it got a bit precarious after a while. Sunset brought into view faint lights across the border. Watching the glittery sparkles made me want to go to Mexico for no other reason than to say, "Yep. I've been there." In my mind, that was reason enough.

"Hey Geoff, do you want to go to Mexico?" I said. "We could wake up and go grab some authentic breakfast tacos, then carry on."

218

"Can we get in? I don't have my passport or anything," he said.

"Yeah, I don't know what you need, but what are they going to say other than, 'No, you can't come in.'" In all reality, that probably wasn't the worst thing that could happen, but all other possibilities never crossed my mind. I also never thought about how we would get back into America. That's where we would need the passport or other credentials. However, I desperately wanted those tacos. *To hell with the consequences, tacos eclipse all.*

After a night at Pancho Villa State Park, we loaded up our gear and set off for Mexico in search of an authentic foreign breakfast. As we slowly pedaled south, my stomach dropped as the border crossing came into view. I had no idea what to expect, and to make matters even more complicated, Geoff and I looked like homeless refugees looking to escape America. We rode our bikes right up to the gate, and with no foreign travel experience to rely on, I was thrown for a loop when the guards didn't speak English. I thought there would be a buffer zone of Spanglish at least, but nope, I sank into the language pool's deep end without a life jacket. *Come on, Spanish 101, don't fail me now.*

I'm not sure if the guard asked for my ID or not, but I handed him my driver's license and then pointed to the taco truck we were going to and said, "Tacos." *That's the best you can do? "Tacos?"*

He pointed to my sleeping bag on my bike and presumably asked what all of my gear was for as he began poking and prodding at my saddlebags. I did my best to mime out "sleep" and "blanket," which must have worked because he handed my ID back and let us through. *Spanish 101 needs to be a two-part class: Spanish and Miming.*

We rode down the main street and got sideswiped by a change in the cultural atmosphere. I'll be the first to admit: I'd had no idea the extreme poverty existing just a mile from where I'd gone to sleep the night prior. I was in culture shock. But I wanted to experience what this little town in Mexico had to offer. With no clue what to do in the situation, I sought out the only thing my stomach would let me do: get tacos.

We rode up to a dusty, run-down little taco truck parked on a street side but then decided, for our gut's health, to find an established restaurant. The bugs and dirt on the taco truck didn't help its case, either. The Pink Store was a two-story building painted pink that looked like the perfect tourist trap, so of course, we went. As we pulled up to the side door of the building, a local offered to watch our bikes for us. Again, I had to utilize my sub-par miming skills to communicate, so it was hard to tell if we were about to get robbed or not. He held out his hand flat and poked the center of his palm with his other index finger, requesting payment for services rendered. We suspiciously agreed, but I only had a Mountain Dew to barter with. He seemed satisfied, so we locked our bikes up, and went inside.

New Mexico

The Pink Store was, in fact, a tourist trap, but it had everything we needed: breakfast tacos (that were the best tacos of my life) and some souvenirs. I really wanted some coffee to go with breakfast, but decided bottled water would be the safer route. The Pink Store was the best we could conjure up for an impromptu visit to a foreign country that ensured we wouldn't get giardia or some other ride-halting illness.

As we approached the gate back into America, the guard waved us toward him. I pulled up alongside the booth and showed the guard my driver's license, and he quickly let us through. To put our border crossing into perspective, it took us ten minutes and a lot of gesturing to get into Mexico and twenty seconds to get back into the United States. Total time in Mexico: 2 hours and 37 minutes.

As we pedaled away from Mexico, I looked back and saw The Pink Store getting smaller in the distance. Thinking back on the people we'd met during our brief Mexico trip, I realized that everyone had been amicable, despite the conditions of poverty. They hadn't fit the stereotypes I'd heard, and had seemed to want to speak with us even though the language barrier was inconvenient, albeit comical. I was only a mile away, but already wanted to go back and experience what Mexico had to offer.

We pedaled alongside the Mexican border on Route 9 for the entire day, until we reached El Paso, and the start of our Texas saga. Total time in New Mexico: 2 days and 7 hours.

Texas

We rolled into El Paso well after dark, as was becoming customary, especially when we had to meet a Warmshowers host. It wasn't for lack of trying, though. We genuinely hated for our hosts to stay up late, waiting for us to arrive. However, we were consistently either overzealous in our goals for the day's ride, dealing with mechanical issues, or battling the unexpected terrain and elements. No matter the reason, we were always behind schedule.

When we finally did meet our hosts for the night, they came out with big smiles and an extremely welcoming demeanor. Richie and Lillie were two of the friendliest people we met on the entire trip. Richie worked at a local bike shop, and Lillie just loved riding every day, so we immediately had common ground, and our conversations never got boring. I believe it was around 10 PM when Richie asked us if we wanted to see the town.

"Uhhh... sure, but it's late, and we've got to ride in the morning," I said.

Richie laughed. "You guys can stay for as long as you want, so there's no need to hurry out in the morning. Plus," he said as he started to grin, "have you ever had a Mexican margarita?"

I chuckled and said, "Isn't that just a margarita?"

"Nope. Come on, let's go out, and I'll show you."

Never one to turn down a midnight adventure, Geoff and I unloaded our bikes into the living room, hopped on our trusty steeds, and rode to Richie's favorite bar. *God, I love riding without any weight on this bike.*

We pulled up to a little dive bar, locked our bikes, and went inside. One look at the bar menu and I could tell that I would love this place. They had all kinds of Mexican food that I had never heard of, so I ended up ordering cow stomach, cow tongue, and some other animal intestines. Every bite was a flavorful mouth bomb that exploded on impact.

At some point, while I was distracted by my food, Richie got up and ordered a round of Mexican margaritas. It turned out that a Tecate beer with a salted rim and a tequila shot constitutes a Mexican margarita. It's customary to shoot the tequila and then chug the beer. If I've learned any-thing in my travels, it's that I love traditions. A couple of cultural practices later, and it was time to head back to Richie and Lillie's place for some sleep.

Richie and Lillie were so much fun to be around that we ended up staying in El Paso for two or three days. Still, we didn't want to overstay our welcome and eventually left, feeling rejuvenated and ready to tackle Texas. But not without first changing my facial hair so I could blend in with the local crowd better. It's common knowledge that every Texan has a handlebar mustache, so I shaved my cheeks and my chin, leaving my face to sport only a mustache that would make Paul Teutul Sr. jealous. It was a horrible look for me, but I donned it with the pride of a cocky jackass. *Let's crush Texas.*

Around sixty miles from El Paso, we stealth camped at Fort Hancock, underneath a set of picnic tables. It wasn't very stealthy, by any means, but we slept fast and woke early to make sure we weren't woken up by the police again.

The next day we paralleled Interstate 10 for a while, until we had no choice but to get on the interstate and ride alongside the eighty-mile-per-hour traffic. It was a miserable day, but we made it to Van Horn. Having to ride beside loud traffic, inhale truck exhaust, and fight high winds and terrible road conditions did not exactly motivate us to sleep on the dirt again, so we got a hotel room.

The next day we set out toward Marfa. Geoff was excited to get there and told me all about how it was a mecca for artists, especially minimalists. As we neared the town, we saw a small building off to the right with two little canopies jutting out of its otherwise rectangular shape. The word "Prada" was printed on the awnings that shaded purses and shoes perched in the windows. There was a door that had no intention of being opened. It had no handle and no push or pull sign, either. The box was just a rectangular building with tiered shelving displays in the windows and "Prada" printed on the awnings. That's it.

Marfa is weird, but in the best possible way.

We rolled into town well after dark. The temperature had long since dropped below freezing, yet again. We planned to stay at a campground near the center of the town, but after we checked their prices, we decided to stay in a hotel since it was only ten dollars more and we could get warm.

Marfa gave me some weird vibes for sure, especially the next day when we stopped and checked out the "Marfa Lights Viewing Area" on the east side of town. The little plaques staged around the viewing area displayed information about the strange lights that appear off the horizon and can be seen from this spot, located just off Highway 90. However, it was noon, so we just read some interesting theories about the lights on the little plaques, ate peanut butter and jelly tortillas, and rode on.

About sixty miles later, we made it to Marathon, Texas, where Richie and Lillie had let us in on a little secret called La Loma del Chivo, an inspiring, industrious-hippie compound where papercrete and upcycled trash was turned into beautiful homes. La Loma del Chivo translated into English is "The Goat's Hill" or "Hill of the Goat." Ingrid Voelkel and Guilford Jones had created del Chivo, as I colloquially referred to it, together with the help of a couple of other folks. Either way, we made a beeline straight for the place, given the wild Campfire Yelp reviews from Richie and Lillie.

La Loma del Chivo had a magical wonderment to it from the moment we arrived. Seeing the brightly painted and uniquely shaped papercrete buildings made me feel like I had stepped into an arid, dusty *Alice in Wonderland*. We were met with big, rapturous smiles at the gate and immediately offered a place to stay. We followed our host to the building, leaned our bikes up against the wall, and walked inside to our room. I crawled onto the top bunk to call it home for the night, still fully dressed from the day's ride, and noticed exposed wiring just inches above my face. *Hmm. That's probably not safe. Oh well, I've seen worse.*

"Goodnight, Geoff," I said as I closed my eyes and slept without a care in the world.

The next morning, I groggily dragged myself into the common area outside our building, where there was a fire pit, some couches, a table, and the kitchen. *An outdoor kitchen. Nice.*

Someone had already gotten the fire going, and Geoff was up, tinkering with his bike per his usual morning routine.

"Dude," I said to Geoff, "I feel like trash. I am so tired."

"Make some coffee," he said like it was no big deal.

We had been friends for nine years at that point, but at that moment, I realized Geoff didn't know that I didn't know how to make coffee. I was a twenty-four-year-old college graduate who had never drunk from, much less made, a pot of homemade coffee in my life.

"OK," I said. "How?"

He smiled and exhaled loudly out of his nose, as if I had made a joke. When he looked up and realized it was a real question, he said, "Just put the grounds in the filter on top of the coffee maker," emphasizing "in the filter." He continued, "Fill up the back part with water, then turn it on. It's easy."

"OK," I said. I turned to the kitchen area and stared at the coffee maker like it was a chemistry set, and I was curing cancer. I was unqualified to be making coffee, but I wanted to help. *What's the worst thing that can happen?*

I grabbed the coffee tin, labeled "Espresso," and filled the filter to the top, making sure to pack it down, so it didn't overflow. I added in more grounds, up to the rim. Then I put water in the back of the machine and turned it on. *Easy.* Nothing had gone wrong, and nothing had broken.

I learned a lot about coffee that day. Espresso is a finely ground coffee meant to deliver a higher concentration of caffeine. Also, I wasn't supposed to fill up the filter to the top, and I definitely wasn't supposed to pack the grounds in. These two mistakes created a sludge that dripped out of the coffee maker like thick, used oil. Once the coffee finished percolating, the liquid concoction barely swirled as I tried moving it around in the decanter. *Oh well, I've drunk worse.*

I poured the coffee into two mugs, each with two sugars. I gave Geoff his and sat down to have my first ever cup of coffee. I sipped it gently. One sip made my eyes water.

Geoff retched immediately. He put his mug down. "Dude, that's gross. I can't drink that."

"Oh, it's not so bad," I said, not wanting to waste my effort. As I drank it again, it got easier and more comfortable to swallow, like a half-melted marshmallow. I eventually finished mine, and as I started to drink Geoff's, a guy named Mike walked up and offered us a morning tour. Mike was all smiles, all the time, and had two long braids coming from his goatee, with the center part of his chin and the rest of his face freshly shaved. I got the sense he genuinely loved being a part of the community there and was excited to show it off. Mike was one of the folks who'd helped build the compound.

By the tour of the third building, I no shit thought I was floating. I genuinely believed that the coffee had been laced with something because my head was spinning and my legs were twitching so fast that I thought I could see time. I had so much energy that I couldn't even move. I had to stay still for fear of taking off running and not knowing how far I would go. I tried listening to my heartbeat, but all I heard was the thunderous drumfire of my insides, giving it all they had to fight off death. *This is it.... This is how I die. Not a bad way to go, I suppose.*

It took the better half of the day, but I finally came down off of what I can only assume was the highest caffeine buzz there has ever been. I don't remember what happened that day, but once I came back to earth, we were still walking around del Chivo. We went into a building with glass bottles sticking through the walls, allowing colorful streams of light to bounce around the inside. It was a beautiful and creative way to recycle and the perfect way for me to detox and reenter the realms of men.

Later that night, we met two guys by the names of Gail and Paul. Gail got the conversation going as we joined them around the fire pit and cracked open a couple of beers. Immediately Gail asked, "But what does it all mean?"

I looked over to Paul, who I assumed had been in a discussion about something with Gail, and saw only Paul staring back at me, waiting for me to reply to Gail's question. Confused, I looked at Gail and asked, "I'm sorry, what does all of what mean?"

"This, man. Us. Here. This place. Why?" He asked as if I knew the answer. *Uhhh... I'm going to need something more potent than a beer to get me through this. Where's that coffee pot?*

"I don't know, man." I said. "Sometimes it just all lines up that way for a reason, I guess."

The four of us took a long pause and gazed into the fire, contemplating whatever it was that had just happened. It was Paul who finally broke the silence and asked us, "So where did y'all come from?"

As we talked about our bike trip, Paul's unimpressed reactions and ability to toss cycling jargon around let me know he was an adventurer himself, so I asked him how he ended up at del Chivo. "Well, I'm on a cross-country cycle tour myself, and I always stay here when I come through," he said. *Nice!* We immediately connected and started talking about gear, tips, tricks, and everything cycle-tour related.

Eventually, his dream to solo-push a car across America on his fortieth birthday came up, and I really didn't know how to respond. It would be a logistical nightmare, and I wanted to throw a hundred questions at him to try and work them out, but then I remembered how that felt at my graduation party, so I let it be. "That would be one hell of an accomplishment. I hope you make it happen," I said and left it at that. A couple of beers later, and it was time for bed.

We woke up early and took off before sunrise. La Loma del Chivo had made an impact on us both in a way that neither of us could describe. We tried figuring out what made that place so unique and captivating, but we couldn't put it into words.

In a perfect world, we would have known what Mother Nature would do, and would have stayed at del Chivo a few more days, but we rode off the next morning, straight into thirty-plus-mile-per-hour headwinds. We were pedaling as hard as we could, and it felt like we were going backward. I'm sure I could have walked faster. As we rode farther away from del Chivo, my hopes to one day return to that enchanted commune grew with every pedal stroke.

It was a grueling day's ride, but fifty-four miles later, we arrived in Sanderson, Texas, population 837. We pulled into a deserted campground. Only two or three campers were in the whole lot, but it didn't look like a terrible place to stay, with a small mountain in the backdrop. I walked up to the tin-roofed office and knocked on the door. A heavy-set man answered, asking if we needed help.

"Um. Yes, we need a place to put up our tent for the night," I said.

"Just one tent? For the both of you?" he asked, looking us up and down inquisitively. "Oooh-kay," he said, raising his eyebrows and avoiding eye contact, "that will be thirty dollars."

I mentally busted out laughing. *He thinks we're going to go Brokeback Mountain out here!* I'm sure they didn't see many guys dressed in spandex, asking to sleep in the same tent, so I let it slide, but for the rest of the week, I would look at Geoff and go, "Oooh-kay" with a slight eye roll and laugh. The experience reminded me that wearing spandex is

233

kind of weird and that when I got home, I would be wearing regular clothes again. Not to mention, I would be sleeping with Kaitlyn again, which would be quite the upgrade from my current sleeping partner. *No offense Geoff. You're just not my type.*

We pitched our tent on the back side of a building that looked more like a horse stable than a campground recreation center, to help mitigate the wind exposure. It did very little. The tent flapped around and made a horrid whipping noise all night, but I was too tired to let it bother me. I listened to it for only a few seconds before I fell asleep, and then a few seconds every hour throughout the night.

We woke up to sprinkling rain. The thunderheads were pretty far off in the distance, so we left quickly to outride the storm before it got any worse. Within minutes, we were on our bikes and pedaling hard toward Langtry. We had gotten used to not having a plan, but trying to outride a storm always made me a bit nervous. It wasn't the rain that bothered me, but knowing that cars couldn't see me in the rain made me feel like an unwanted target. Luckily, traffic wasn't too bad, and we had to deal with only the occasional car splashing us.

But we weren't fast enough to outrun the storm, and the slight rain turned into hail. *What the hail?!* I laughed maniacally with absolutely no prompt from anyone, which made Geoff give me an odd look.

"What the hail," I said in anticipation of thunderous

laughter.

A slight shake of the head was all I got, but I started laughing again anyway. We were in the middle of the desert, getting pelted by pebble-sized hail, and had nowhere to take shelter. There was nothing around for as far as we could see, which made the whole experience even funnier because it could have gotten no worse. Of course, that's when the bumpy asphalt turned into almost unrideable gravel. *Great.* (The road conditions fluctuated from bad to worse so much in Texas that my left hand started to lose feeling in the pinky and ring fingers. I wondered if I was doing permanent damage, or if this was just something to make me temporarily uncomfortable.)

It finally quit hailing as we arrived in Langtry. We wasted no time finding a spot to sleep, giving us time to do some housekeeping. We had to hang everything up to dry, do some routine maintenance on our bikes, and try to stay warm. The spot we picked in the bushes, just off the side of the road, was a perfect place to call home for the evening.

We woke up to more rain. *Sweet. I'm so glad all of our stuff is lying out to dry.* As I got out of the tent to put on my cold, wet clothes, I wanted to get on the bike and ride as fast as I could to get out of the weather, but I just wasn't feeling strong. I looked over and noticed Geoff was a bit sluggish, getting out of the tent, which was unusual for him.

"You OK?" I asked.

"Not really. I think I'm going to..." was all Geoff

could say before his vomit landed just inches from the tent.
Gross.

"Well, let's get going," he said. "I don't want to stay here another night. We've got to keep moving."

With my eyebrows raised in shock, I said, "OK. Let's go."

When I have a sudden rush of adrenaline, I love how everything moves so slowly that I can notice the most minute details. I can see the wrinkles on someone's face as they take a punch at me. I can notice the rust on the hubcaps of a car that almost runs into me. It's the smallest, most insignificant things that stand out. When we were riding that day, I noticed how the sand on the side of the road overlapped the speckled gravel like waves at a beach. I saw this because an F-350 pushed me off the road, and I was crashing.

The truck passed so close to me that his draft pulled me toward him. I leaned to my right and tried to stay on the road while not being hit, but there wasn't enough room on the road. I had to practice my off-roading skills onto some bricks that had been smashed into tiny pieces years ago. As the truck went past, I continued to ride over the brick remnants, trying my best to pull back onto the road. I made it to inches from the asphalt and had almost fully recovered when my front tire slammed into a rock and stopped. My back tire, with fifty pounds of gear on it, lifted off the ground. I was falling to my left side, into the road and into more traffic. I put my left hand down to brace for impact and crashed into the gravel-strewn road. My hand hit first, followed by my shoulder, then head. The helmet cracked and then scraped along on the asphalt. An odd sensation shot through my arm, but I couldn't tell what it was. I was waiting for the pain to set in, but it never did.

The cars went around me and kept on driving. Better than the alternative of driving through me, I suppose. My leg had somehow managed to become intertwined in the bike frame, making it hard to untangle myself and get up. I finally stood up just as Geoff made it back to me. Geoff first noticed the blood on my knee, and that's when I felt the dull pain. It wasn't too bad, though, just a good bump and a bit of blood. I'd picked my bike up to inspect the damage when vertigo took over. I slowed down to better check my body.

My hand. *Oh fuck. I can't feel half of my hand.* I squeezed my fist and shook it about in a mild panic, wanting to feel something, but nothing happened. There was gravel stuck in my hand where it had hit the ground on the outside of my palm. *Oh shit. Oh shit. Oh shit.* No feeling was worse than no pain. Pain I knew. Pain was a familiar friend. This was unnerving, and I wanted my friend to come back.

My helmet had a long crack down the side, but my head seemed fine. My knee was bloody, but I could still use it. My hand was numb but still moveable. My bike was scratched, but that just gave it character. There was nothing I could do about any of the damage.

"Let's go, Geoff," I said. "I can still ride."

We made it thirty miles to Comstock before deciding to quit pushing it. We got a motel, and I was asleep before sunset.

The past couple of days, we had dealt with thirty-plus-mile-per-hour headwinds, gotten hailed on, felt under the weather, and now had a wreck to top it off. The road conditions were the worst we'd seen on the trip. I'd crashed and lost all feeling in three fingers and half of my hand, all with the bonus of cold rain and unexpected rolling hills. It had been three days of terrible riding, but the morning we woke up in Comstock, everything changed.

We walked outside the motel to sunny skies, seventy-five degrees, and a slight breeze. It was picture perfect. The shoulder of the road got smoother and wider too. The wind kicked up a bit, but it was at our backs, nudging us along all day. It had been a tough couple of days, but I would have done it all again to experience that moment. Three days of misery for one absolutely perfect day, where nothing went wrong, is a fair trade in my book. That night we slept at a rest area off the road, and I distinctly remember hearing crickets for the first time in months. As I gently swung back and forth in the hammock, underneath the covered picnic area, I stared out into the surrounding shrubbery and felt entirely at ease, without a care in the world, listening to the crickets. *Welcome home, Shaun. You made it back to the South.*

Texas was infinitely hillier than I ever could have

imagined. We started the day ignorantly riding into what was regionally known as "hill country." We had grown soft and used to riding down the continental divide's back end, and now we had to deal with mind-numbing hill repeats. As my head hung down and I pushed through the pain in my legs, I could almost hear Paul from Germany saying, "The mountains are the most honest thing I've ever met. Hills are lying bastards that change their minds quickly."

It was true. I was mentally struggling with the hills because, for some reason, I honestly thought that Texas was pancake flat. It was my ignorance that caused my disappointment, which had turned into frustration, but it was something I had to get over. We rode those hills for days, passing through small, quaint Texas towns, and it all seemed to blur together. It wasn't until Kerrville that I realized Southern hospitality was still alive and that I needed to appreciate each of these towns for what it was.

We rode into Kerrville late that night. The temperature was above freezing, so not terrible, but my clothes were soaked in sweat from the day's ride. We stopped at a McDonalds so I could enjoy my newfound addiction to warm coffee. While we sat at a booth, I tucked my arms into my shirt to get warm. The scruffy, bearded man next to us asked us what we were doing riding at night.

As we kicked up the conversation, we told him we had gotten a late start that day, and we were riding late into the night to make up time, but that the nighttime cold wasn't the most fun thing. He said, "Wait right here. I'll be right back." Geoff and I looked at each other oddly and then at the guy's two-year-old child, who he had just left at the booth. We sipped our coffee in silence.

A few minutes later, he came back with a sweatshirt.

"Here you go. It's a bit small for me, but probably a bit big for you," he said with a big laugh. He was right, the sweatshirt went to my knees and made me look like a child, but I was immediately warm. I couldn't thank him enough. I wore that sweatshirt every night for the rest of the trip.

One hundred and fifteen miles from Kerrville is Austin, perhaps the weirdest, kindest, and most authentically kooky city in America. We rode into Austin on a bike path after dark. The trail was all to ourselves for hours, not seeing a single person, but about fifteen miles from the center of the city, a pair of bicycle headlights came straight at us. As we got closer, the headlights slowed down. That was when we met our Austin hosts.

We stopped and asked them where the trail would dump us out if we followed it to the end. The two cyclists were extremely helpful in giving directions and even a short-cut. We ended up chatting a bit about what to do in Austin when stranger number one changed the subject and asked, "Where are y'all coming from?"

"We're coming from... uhh, I can't remember where we stayed last night, but we're riding across America," I said.

"Yeah, I figured. I noticed your setup and how much gear y'all have. Where are y'all staying for the night?"

"Umm..." I gave Geoff a questioning look. "We have no idea."

"Well, if you guys want, we're heading to a friend's house outside of town for the weekend. You can totally stay at our house until we get back. If you want to stay the whole weekend, we would love to chat about how your trip has been so far and take y'all out on the town," said stranger number one as he wrote down their address. "The key is under the ceramic rooster on the left side of the house."

What is happening right now?! This is the strangest, yet nicest thing I've ever experienced.

We talked for a few more minutes and as the conversation came to an end we started riding away, but abruptly stopped, having forgotten to formally introduced ourselves. "I'm Shaun and this is Geoff," I said, shaking my head and smiling, dumbfounded that I was about to sleep in their house and I didn't even know their names. "Thanks for letting us stay at your place for the weekend. We really needed a place to relax for a bit, and can't thank you enough."

"No worries man, I'm Elwood and this is Mae," he said with an understanding smile and head nod. "Have a good time and hopefully we will see y'all later."

We found their house, and the key was where they'd said. *Ooo-kay... Well, we're about to get murdered or have a great night's sleep. What's behind door number one?*

We walked into their house, and it was straight out of a 2012 hipster-rustic-chic magazine. Hanging from the pitched ceiling were hundreds of paper-link chains, clearly the work of a teacher's students. Mustache and bicycle trinkets covered the shiplap walls. The open, outdoor shower in the backyard, with walls of translucent glass, was something new to me but looked relaxing nonetheless. An open-shelf concept in the kitchen made finding everything to make breakfast the next morning convenient. The loft had a futon that reminded me of my college years and made sleep that night a bit rough, but I didn't mind. I was happy to have a place to rest. It had been a rough couple of days, but the kindness of Elwood and Mae was rejuvenating.

We were slow to get up the next morning. Sleeping in had become rare, and it was a nice change of pace. We spent the day relaxing, taking care of our bicycles, reading, and watching TV. It wasn't until the sun went down that we decided to walk around Austin. Dinner was our first stop, at El Corto, a converted short bus that served the second most delicious tacos I think I'd ever eaten. Two bites into the meal, an average-sounding band started playing, but the tambourine player made an unexpected "caaaaaawwwww" screech. Geoff struggled to not spit out his food from laughter, and I had to bite my tongue to keep a straight face. For weeks after that, "caaaaaawwwww" became our motivational war cry whenever there was a lull in conversation or when we became a bit delusional from the day's ride. I may have even had a couple of obnoxiously loud war cry outbursts while shopping for Gatorades in a gas station to see if Geoff could keep a straight face.

After tacos at El Corto, we walked around Austin for a bit and stumbled onto a pizza spot that looked like a place the Teenage Mutant Ninja Turtles frequented. It was run-down, had flickering lights on the outside, and had so many stickers on the outdoor patio, that we could barely see the pillars and picnic tables.

"Yelp says it has four stars," Geoff said.

"We've eaten at worse spots for sure," I said, remembering all the roach coaches and dive bars we'd survived.

I ordered a full large pizza, planning on eating a slice or two, then taking the rest back to the house. When Geoff finished his personal pan pizza, I was still eating, but I didn't want him to wait on me, so we started walking. I ended up eating the whole pizza before we made it back to the house. I felt like I was making up for all those calories lost from days of peanut butter and jelly tortillas, oatmeal, and an everyday favorite, rice and beans. The actual food was comforting. Austin, with all its strange quirks, was comforting. I was getting closer and closer to home, and that too, was comforting.

When we got back to the house that night, I spent a lot of time writing in my journal and thinking about everything I had learned on the trip. What started out as a thoughtful journey of introspection, slowly morphed into me thinking about my future. *What am I going to do when I get home? How am I going to pay my bills, or even more daunting, my student loans? Is Kaitlyn going to let me keep my stuff in her house? Wait, are we officially living together? Am I going to become a teacher or work at camp again? Maybe I can get my old job at Books-a-Million back.* The questions kept piling on, but the answers never came, at least not that night.

We spent two more nights at that house, including one with our hosts. Elwood was a civil engineer in charge of redesigning all the bike paths and trails in Austin. He gave us a history lesson about bike-friendly countries in Europe and how World War II had created a gas shortage. Many European countries responded to the gas shortage by creating "no drive" days, usually on the weekends. Having no cars opened up the roads for people to play football, have community picnics, and just have a generally open space that had previously been taken up by vehicles. After the war, the general population saw the value of bicycles and the importance of separating bikes from cars. Their solution was to create an entire bicycle highway system throughout the cities. It was Elwood's dream to have a bicycle infrastructure that was safe and convenient enough for the everyday bike rider to use. He told us this story with a passion and determination that I usually don't see when people describe their jobs.

Mae was an early childhood educator, which explained the finger paintings and paper chains throughout the living room. She seemed to enjoy her job, too, but once we got to talking about art, that's when the passion came alive in her eyes. She was a creator who loved all things unique and inspiring. I could tell Geoff enjoyed being around another artist. Like-minded people getting along isn't unusual, I suppose.

One evening I noticed that Mae had a brass paper fastener wrapped around her ring finger. I didn't think that she and Elwood were married, but I glanced at Elwood's ring finger and saw a ring made of braided paper. "Hey Elwood, that's a cool idea for a ring. What made you want to do that?" I asked.

Elwood looked up from the magazine he was reading and smiled. "Mae and me have never really subscribed to the idea of marriage, so a few years back we made rings for each other out of random things. Whenever the ring gets old and falls off or breaks, we get an opportunity to reassess our relationship. We ask ourselves things like if we're happy, if this is where we want to be in life, and do we want to stay with each other? We've been together for about eight years now and we still answer those questions with a resounding yes, every time."

I sat back on the couch to let that idea sink in for a moment. *That is beautiful.*

Overall it was refreshing to see two people, with such big hearts, trying to make their community a better place. That's what this country will forever need. Ordinary people, doing ordinary things for the good of their communities.

I'll never forget the kindness and sense of pride that the people of Austin showed us. It will forever be a weird place, and that's precisely how it should stay. *Keep Austin weird.*

We left Austin rejuvenated and ready to ride harder than we ever had. Five hundred miles over the next five days was our goal, and we were eager to get after it.

Five Hundred Miles In Five Days

Day one of our five-century challenge was a success. Not much happened during the bike ride, other than neck cramps, a sore butt, and of course, more oatmeal. We made it ninety-seven miles to Brenham, Texas, but couldn't stop to enjoy the town because we hadn't reached one hundred miles yet. As soon as Geoff's odometer hit one hundred miles, we looked for a place to camp. We were incredibly hungry, and it was already dark, of course. *I am only afraid of the dark when I'm hungry, and that's because I'm afraid I won't be able to find food because it's dark.*

Luckily, we couldn't have found a better place to stop if we'd tried.

We were passing what looked like a shed with big red letters above it that read "BBQ." I immediately hit the brakes and pulled over, making Geoff nearly crash into my rear tire.

"Dude," I said. "Let's eat here and figure out where we can sleep for the night."

Without any qualms, Geoff agreed.

We opened the faded wooden door to the sound of squeaky hinges. Two dusty cowboys sat at a wooden table on the opposite side of the room beside a big-screen TV from the 90s. The tension was palpable as they stared us down. I fully expected a gruffy man with a ten-gallon hat to walk out from the back of the restaurant with his pistol on his hip and his boot spurs making a tinging noise as he sauntered closer to us. The lone employee, performing the roles of waitress, cook, and cashier, broke the silence.

"Have a seat anywhere you'd like," she said, drawing out the vowels.

We sat at the only other table in the shed/restaurant and ordered what we would soon find out was some of the best BBQ around.

A couple of quiet, tense minutes passed before the cowboys invited us to their table. They wanted to chat about our odd clothing choice. We obliged, and within minutes they bought us our first Lonestar beers, which they called "the unofficial, official beer of Texas." We were about three officials into the conversation when one of them said, "Hey, have you boys ever seen Jesus?"

Now, growing up Southern Baptist, I thought I knew

where this was heading and said, "I know him, but I've never seen him." A slight grin came across each of their faces.

"He's right outside. I swear. Let me show you," one of them said.

I tensed up a bit, but I figured if weird turned into bad, I could easily outrun them, so we went outside to find Jesus.

"Look right there at that tree," he said. "Jesus is in that tree right there."

It took me a second, but right hand across my heart, Jesus's face was in that tree. A full-grown, thirty-something-year-old male with a full beard was looking straight back at me from that tree. It was weird, but it happened. Just like people see Mary in burnt toast, I saw Jesus in the gnarled wood of a tree.

I figured that was probably the pinnacle moment for the evening, so it was time to find a place to sleep. I asked the employee if there was anywhere we could sleep for the night, and she said, "Sure, you can camp behind this building if you want." *Perfect.* Day one of five was a success. Hopefully, day two would be just as easy.

We'd wanted to wake up and get on the road before the sun was up, but the beers and overall soreness had other plans. We finally got around to riding at 9 AM and ended up riding the majority of the day in a horrible rainstorm. It made for a mind-numbing day, but at least it was mostly flat. There were only a few hills that day, and despite the rain and wind, I was grateful.

Once the sun went down, the clouds parted to reveal a full moon, which made night riding much easier. I could see every pothole and nail on the road just by the moonlight. The temperate weather with straight, flat roads and a full moon made me want to ride all night. That's when I heard what sounded like thunder, except it didn't stop. I looked over my shoulder and saw a herd of horses and cows running with us along their fence line. It was surreal. The moonlight cut through their dust storm, highlighting the herd's leaders and making silhouettes out of the rest. They stayed with us for at least a mile before a fence cut them off. I made a vow never to forget that feeling of awe. It was perfect.

We stopped at a gas station in Mosshill that night, where we met an employee named Garrett who randomly offered to feed us potatoes and hamburgers. *I can't believe this Texan hospitality.* We talked with him for a while before he said we could sleep behind the gas station in a field. For whatever reason, it was some of the most peaceful sleep I had gotten in a while.

We woke up in the middle of that field behind the gas station to a sunny day. It was weird to be camped there, but I was getting used to weird. Seeing the truckers and gas station customers staring at us was uncomfortable, but it reminded me that what Geoff and I were doing wasn't normal. We were on a push to get closer to home and the return to normal, but after the gratifying past couple of days, I struggled with the idea of stopping. I wasn't sure I wanted to go back to normal. *I want to do this forever.*

The idea of riding a bicycle for the rest of my life seemed like a novel idea, but when things were at their best, it was easy to forget the hardships that had come before. I was not ready to ride forever, and the following day would prove it.

We'd left Austin with the goal of completing five hundred miles in five days. Day one, we rode 103 miles. Day two, we rode 108 miles. Day three, we rode a total of eighty miles, finishing the day just across the border into Louisiana. We reached the Gulf of Mexico and knew that if we kept the water on our right for the next 500 miles or so, we would be heading in the right direction.

Geoff and I had set and accomplished so many goals on this trip already that not making this one was readily justifiable in our minds. We said things like, "Ah, we just said five hundred miles in five days, we didn't say a century a day," or, "Who cares if we don't make it the full hundred miles? It's just a number we set to make it to the finish line faster."

Laziness is all about perspective. I have never thought that riding a hundred miles in a day was easy and it's certainly not lazy to ride eighty. However, cutting the distance short because of a nagging thought in my mind, or because riding in the dark was boring, or a discomfort setting in, well, that's laziness. It's easy to justify laziness when discomfort starts setting in. Deciding to push harder than the mind or body wants to go is what separates those who complete their goals from those that justify their failures. In total humility, I admit that I justified my discomfort, decided not to stick to my word, and failed to complete five centuries in five days.

That night, I'm not sure I had ever been more scared to go to sleep in my life.

We're going to die. I'm going to be sleeping in this canvas coffin, and an alligator will calmly walk up and eat me. There was no doubt in my mind that that would happen, but as nervous as I was, I reminded myself that we were only three states from the finish line. I was eager to be home and to sleep in my bed, and I know Geoff was feeling the same way. We had pedaled for three months now, and Christmas was right around the corner. If we didn't make it home for Christmas, our families would kill us, unless of course the alligators beat them to it.

Pedaling through the Rockefeller Wildlife Refuge on Louisiana's coast earlier that day had been a surreal experience. The road was like one giant trail leading straight through a gator breeding ground. It seemed like we were riding on a floating highway in the middle of a swamp. Geoff and I saw more than a few gator slide marks, where the giant reptiles slid into the water over and over again, which meant they were probably nearby. Not only that, but we also spotted the bodies of gators that hadn't made it across the road before a semi truck, or a Louisiana good ole boy F-250, obliterated it. It was apparent the gator population around there was not hurting at all, and I was super nervous about it.

We pedaled for eighty-five miles that day through the swampland, and it only grew more surreal as night came. No way was I going to stop in the middle of the night and walk around looking for a place to sleep. *Hell no. Nope.* Knowing my luck, I would pitch my tent on a gator nest full of eggs. The momma gator would laugh at my stupidity and tell the babies to hatch and have their way with me. *Keep pedaling.*

About an hour after I wanted to stop, we finally started seeing signs of civilization around a place called Pecan Island. Of course, Geoff's compulsive nature wanted to make it one hundred miles. *Dude, we're close enough. Those were the first houses we've seen in hours.* Again, trying to justify my laziness.

I saw an opening in a field to my right. The moonlight shone through the trees like a beacon calling me to bed. I wasn't sure how I picked up the less-than-subtle cues of Geoff's disdain about stopping there. Was it the "Dude, let's keep going!?" that he kept repeating while we walked around the open area, or was it his pessimistic obsession with the spongy weeds that compressed about six inches when we stepped on them? I guess I was in tune with his dislikes by then.

I won the battle, and we ended up pitching the tent on the worst possible weed/grass entanglement ever, all the while getting destroyed by mosquitoes so enormous that when we smacked our legs to kill them, it looked like a bullet wound. By the time we'd finished setting up camp, I looked like a machine gun victim.

Wiping the blood off my arm, I walked toward the road to take a goodnight pee. About ten seconds after the stream had commenced, I saw, standing probably twenty feet in front of me across the street, a man walking to get his newspaper. *This is how I get arrested. Peeing.* I turned around and finished dehydrating quickly. He turned back to go inside his house, having no idea I was there.

I took two steps toward the tent and smacked a mosquito on my arm. *Eff this.* My frustration from the mosquitoes made me risk a trespassing charge, but I didn't care. I turned to face the man and called out to him.

"Sir! Is it OK for us to camp here for the night?"

The man turned around, stared into the dark woods for a second and then finally saw a 5'9" male in spandex standing in the middle of the Louisiana swamp. A look of bewilderment flooded his face.

To break the awkward silence I said, "Me and my buddy are cycling across America and need a place to stay for the night. Is it cool if we sleep in this field across from your house?"

"Sure. That's fine." He said it like it was an everyday occurrence and the look of bewilderment melted from his face almost immediately. "Y'all hungry? I've got some low country boil if y'all wanna eat." The man's voice was as creole as they come.

No freaking way! I looked back at Geoff and saw he was eavesdropping on my conversation. With a bit of pensiveness, Geoff agreed to go inside a stranger's house and eat a stranger's food with me. Not just food, but low country boil, which is one of my favorite foods. Shrimp, corn, sausage, potatoes, mussels, and occasionally crabs, covered in Old Bay and boiled until the potatoes are done.

We secured everything at camp and walked on over to his house. He invited us in the door, and it smelled like a personal seafood buffet. I couldn't believe he had cooked that much food for himself. And then it just so happened that two bottomless pits were riding by in the middle of the night. It was perfect.

The man asked us scores of questions about our adventure while Geoff and I ate the best meal we'd had in a while. After the questions died down, he asked if he could turn the TV on, and sure enough, we ended up watching *Swamp People.* I had no objections, but it was my turn to start asking him questions about swamp life. We ended up talking for hours.

I thanked him as much as I could and still don't believe that my gratitude showed entirely. We left the house laughing and with full bellies, not even slightly upset that we were returning to the mosquitoes' playground. I couldn't have thought of a better way to end a hundredish-mile day.

Geoff and I often talked about how much we had changed from Seattle to Louisiana. Getting up early enough to have camp packed up, bikes loaded, and breakfast eaten all before the sun came up was now the norm, a far cry from three months prior when we would just be getting on the road by noon or later. We learned to live like animals in the savanna, exerting energy only when the sun was not melting our brains. On the days that Geoff would deem "hot," it made sense to cycle when it was cooler during the morning and evening, making the whole day more enjoyable, unless it was 20 degrees in the morning. Those days I hated, but I had to keep reminding myself that nothing was as intensely awful as that ride that had led to my breakdown in Nevada. I would (hopefully) never be that fiercely cold again.

Once we had become accustomed to touring, we never purposefully waited for the day to warm up to start riding. We knew we needed to put miles under our tires and would deal with the cold to get down the road. We started late more than once due to over-indulging, but that was justifiable in our minds. *I gotta stay hydrated.*

Far from a freezing morning, it was only a bit chilly the day after our low country boil meal, making me slow to get up early, but Geoff was always more disciplined and awake before me. Before I could wipe the drool off my face, he had already packed his bags, so naturally, my guilt forced me into indignantly packing my own bags. We were on the road within minutes, but our oatmeal supply was running low, thank God, and we hadn't eaten yet. We stopped at a gas station after about ten miles to fuel up on the usual: muffins, chips, Honey Buns, and Gatorade.

While Geoff was picking out what kind of peanuts he wanted, I kicked up a conversation with the cashier, who, in proper Louisiana form, was wearing her *Swamp People* T-shirt.

"Oh man, Troy and Liz," I said. "They are my favorite people on that show by far."

She laughed like that was the funniest thing she had heard all week. "Liz is my aunt," she said.

I began rambling on with nonsense about how cool that was and asking a myriad of questions trying to figure out if Liz and Troy disliked each other in real life or if it was for the show.

"I can call her up and see if she wants to come down here if you want," the cashier said, most likely annoyed by my rapid-fire questions.

"That would be awesome!" *Oh man, I'm about to meet a bonafide celebrity. I should have shaved this handlebar mustache, showered in the past week, or at least washed my spandex.* I looked haggard, but I was ecstatic.

We waited for maybe ten minutes before Liz walked into the gas station like she owned the place. All smiles and extremely welcoming, she shook our hands, and it was like we had known each other for years. Liz's mom was there, too, and just like a true Southerner, she tried to feed us some of her homemade pickled okra. This was the first time I'd ever had pickled okra, but I ate nearly the whole jar.

Liz, her mom, Geoff, and I traded cycling stories for gator stories until it was almost lunchtime. I knew we had a long day ahead of us, but I figured there will always be another day to ride one hundred miles, but this was my one day to meet Liz, so I didn't worry about missing the ride.

After we took fanboy pictures and started riding away, I realized that I had watched *Swamp People* on the plane ride from Boston to Seattle, then again the previous night, and then I had met Liz. *Wild*.

On day five of five of our hundred-miles-per-day challenge, we rode thirty-nine miles and slept in another shed at a big box home improvement store. We had already failed the challenge, but that's cycle touring; sometimes, it's better to see where the day will take you than to force the day into something it's not.

Overall, it was a challenging goal that showed us we weren't superhuman, and that is a lesson I need to be re-taught, continually.

The Rest Of Louisiana

Is this entire state made up of swamps and waterways? Highway 90 was a series of bridges that went on for miles and weaved its way through a couple of small towns. We were on one of those long bridges somewhere around the city of Gray when a gentleman who spoke broken English pulled his truck over to the side of the bridge, got out, and offered us water. *This is super nice, but a bridge probably isn't the best place to stop and chat.* We accepted the water and started riding again. The bridge was too narrow for Geoff and me to ride side by side, so I was left alone to process the kindness that had just happened. *What made him pull over and risk getting hit by cars to give us water? What made him assume we needed water? Why aren't more people like this?* My mind tried to answer the surge of questions while my body tried to keep up with Geoff, who was pedaling harder now for some reason.

I enjoyed my time on the West Coast and then shortly thereafter in the dusty desert, but I had missed the South and the kind of hospitality it's known for. I looked out into the ominous swampland and saw two beautiful white egrets flying along with us. *I love it here.*

It was getting close to 10 PM when we finally made it to the outskirts of New Orleans. One of the few good things about riding at night was rolling into a well-lit city, where we could see where we were going. The downside to riding in a city was the traffic, even late at night.

We found a small gas station just outside the Crescent City and pulled over to fuel up on Gatorade and Honey Buns, but more importantly, to rest up a bit before the heart-pumping city traffic started. I listened to some music for a bit while we loitered around the parking lot. When a song by Maylene and the Sons of Disaster came on, I got the urge to start moshing but managed to restrain all except my head, which banged ever so slightly. As the chorus played, I couldn't help but think about my own life and how the song was perfectly fitting.

>(Let's go down into the water)
>Hear the choir on the shoreline sing
>(The Mississippi ain't the river Jordan)
>It won't wash me clean

The words got me thinking about the South and how

I had been embarrassed to call myself southern for so long. Of course, we do not have the best history, the best educational record, or the best of anything that I was striving for in my life at the time, but I realized I had desperately missed the South and everything it has to offer. Sweet tea, southern hospitality, genuine people, and the best food on the planet, to name a few things I loved and missed about home. I needed to metaphorically baptize myself in the Mississippi, the river that has practically defined the South, to get back to my roots, even though it wouldn't make me clean.

After we finished our sugary dinner, we got on our bikes and headed toward downtown New Orleans. Less than a mile down the road, we passed a sign saying we were about to cross the Mississippi River. *Well, that's weird.*

We started up the steep incline on the bridge, dodging the ridiculous amount of trash and debris on the road while maneuvering around gigantic drainage covers with gaps wide enough that my bicycle tire would fall straight through them. The bridge was under construction too, shutting the left lane down and forcing every car to ride in the right lane. Every car that passed us had to make the decision to either scrape their car against the traffic barrels on the left side of the lane, or to bump us up against the concrete barrier. I started breathing heavily and demanding more from my legs as cars passed within inches of us. *This sucks. This sucks. Shit. This sucks.* I looked over my shoulder to check for a car.

Fuck! My tire sank straight into the drainage grate.

The whole front end of my bicycle fell out from underneath me, ripping the handlebars from my hands. I lurched over my handlebars, my feet still clipped into my pedals, bringing the rest of my bike with me. The front fork slammed into the metal grate, as my bags, my body, and the rest of my bicycle flew upside down over my front tire. I landed on my head and shoulder as my bike crashed down on top of me, scraping the small concrete barrier that was the only thing between me and falling off the bridge.

I ignored the sharp pain shooting down my neck because I knew what I needed to do. *Get up! Get up now!* I violently kicked my legs to unclip my feet and untangle myself from my bike frame. I managed to get free and began crawling out from under my bike, but I couldn't see anything because a car's headlights blinded me. *The car! Oh shit!* I threw myself into the concrete barrier as the car flew past me. I looked back to check for another one. *No cars. Move now!* Not caring about anything other than getting to safety, I grabbed the seat post and pulled my bike across the traffic lane, taking refuge behind the construction cones. I stumbled to safety behind the cones, put my hands on my knees, and struggled to breathe. When I looked up, my water bottle was rolling down the bridge. I walked toward it, only then seeing the car coming full speed toward me.

I jumped out of the way, back behind the cones, and laughed, screamed, and barely withheld tears as the adrenaline rush became too much. I couldn't think clearly enough to even cross the street without almost killing myself. I needed to get off of the bridge, and quickly.

I had completely forgotten about Geoff until he appeared beside me. He calmly stepped out into the road when there were no cars coming to get my water bottle as I inspected my bike. There were some scrapes on the frame, my handlebar tape looked like someone had taken a cheese grater to it, and my brakes were now parallel to the ground, but I ignored all the aesthetic problems and got off the bridge as quickly as I could. Foregoing the traffic lane full of nails and gaping holes in the concrete, we got back into the right-hand lane and pedaled as fast as possible until we were off the bridge. *That was not the baptism I was expecting.*

As we rode away from the bridge, I remember thinking, "I almost fell off of a bridge and got hit by a car... twice." I was shaking from the adrenaline and could barely ride at a steady pace. I was either sprinting through downtown, so amped up from the epinephrine, or barely moving forward, hardly able to move the pedals from a lack of energy. The farther into New Orleans we got, the more my adrenaline wore off, and I knew I was about to mentally crash. We had to keep riding because our Warmshowers host was expecting us. Well, sort of expecting us.

Every Warmshowers host was different, and every experience was different, but I vividly remember our host in New Orleans. I remember being overly comfortable in an uncomfortable, uncustomary situation.

Geoff and I normally contacted our host when we got within thirty minutes of their house, to let them know we were nearby. And so, in keeping with the courteous tradition, we called our New Orleans host to let him know we were close.

"Cool," he said. "Just hop the fence and pitch your tent in the yard."

"OK," I said, a little taken aback at being told to hop a fence. It was off-putting, but nothing was off limits at that point. I needed a place to come down off my adrenaline rush, and fast.

"Dude, we can't hop a fence," Geoff said. "This sounds a bit too sketchy. Let me call him back real quick." I obliged since I was sure Geoff didn't want to look like a balking bicycling burglar.

Our host admitted he had given us his friend's address and assumed his friend would be cool with us staying there. It turned out even I had a comfort line that I was not willing to cross. We told him we would find somewhere else to stay. He paused to think and reluctantly gave us his own address.

A short while later, we rolled up to his home in the middle of what I would call New Orleans suburbia, which was a bunch of houses crammed next to each other on tiny streets. A man was outside, moving stuff around on his lawn. I called out and asked if he was our host.

He said, "I was getting worried you guys weren't

coming."

"We had a little incident on the bridge coming over here," I said. *And we were given the wrong damn address, to begin with.* "Sorry we're late."

"No worries. Just set your tents up on the lawn anywhere. I'll go get us some beers." He walked inside.

We realized he hadn't been up-front with us because he was already hosting a touring cyclist and had not wanted to overextend his hospitality. The other cyclist's gear was set up in the yard, but they had left to go explore the city for the night.

Our host came out with the nightcaps and handed me one. That's when I noticed his tattoo-covered hands. He had gauged ears and a punk rock T-shirt on. He made very little small talk but did mention that he had to get up for work early in the morning, so we probably wouldn't be seeing much of him, which was fine with me since I needed sleep, badly.

I knew it was going to be a weird day when I opened my eyes and saw Geoff still asleep. The morning breath had filled the tiny tent so I quietly scrambled to get out into the fresh air. I was so intently focused on being quiet that I nearly screamed when I saw the other cycle tourist just feet away from me, eating oatmeal. *I'm glad I'm not the only one being subjected to this oat soup every day, but dang man, back up. It's creepy.*

Geoff woke up shortly after and we started talking to

the other tourist, mostly about what he had learned were the locals' favorite spots. With the full intention of staying another night, we took off on our bikes to explore the city for the day. We enjoyed the leisurely, saddlebag-free afternoon by riding around Bourbon Street. We smoked cigars, saw some Mardi Gras beads being earned, and had a couple of beers. Of course, since we were in New Orleans, we had to get some creole lunch, and luckily our host had pointed us to his favorite spot before heading off to bed the night before.

It took us a while, but we found the small, local hole-in-the-wall, right in the middle of Bourbon Street. We sat to check out the menu, and just as I picked up the laminated lunch list, I heard a loud, dull smack. It sounded like a pumpkin splattering after being dropped from a ladder. I looked outside to find the source of the sound.

An older woman had tripped on the cobblestone street and landed, head first, on the sidewalk. The blood was pooling next to her face so fast that it looked fake, like someone had a gallon of dark red paint and was pouring it beside her. I stood and started toward her. I yelled at someone to grab napkins to help stop the bleeding. A crowd began to gather around her.

Someone yelled, "I'm an EMT! Get out of the way!" I backed away. I know a fair bit about first aid and CPR, having majored in kinesiology and physical education. Still, I let the EMT do his job because the old military adage always rings true: "lead, follow, or get out of the way." This was undoubtedly a get out of the way moment.

He rolled her over to her side and pressed some napkins and cloth against her head. He checked her eyes and her breathing, kept her talking, and kept her stable on her side until the ambulance arrived five minutes later.

Geoff and I sat in silence, processing what had happened, until a girl walked up and asked us what we thought about the whole thing. *What am I supposed to say? That I could have just watched someone die, and now I'm supposed to look forward to my sandwich? That the blood on the EMT could have diseases and that his quick reaction could have saved her life but endangered his?*

"That was crazy. I hope she's OK," was all I said.

We packed our tent and mounted our bikes in New Orleans the next morning with heavy hearts, hoping she would make a full recovery. With nothing more we could do, we rode.

We never unpacked our tent again. We were determined to make it home before Christmas, and setting up camp wasted time. It was time to focus on riding.

We rode fifty-three miles that day to Waveland, Louisiana. We stopped at a gas station a little past the town to fuel up before looking for a hotel. As I opened my Honey Bun, a disheveled man in ragtag clothing approached us and asked where we were going.

"Oh, we're just headed down the road to a hotel for

the night," I said. "We're tired of camping for right now."

"Right on da beach!" he yelled. "You can stay right on da beach!"

As much as the yelling startled me, I couldn't help but focus on his wild hand gestures and the spit flying from his mouth.

"Oh yeah?" I asked. "Where on the beach?"

He leaned in as if he was going to tell us a secret. "Right on the beach," he whispered.

He continued with some other slurred rantings until a police officer approached us. The unkempt gentleman said a sentence or two more, excused himself, and walked off down the street.

The police officer said, "Yeah, he likes to hang around here a lot and ask people for money. We've had a couple of drug-related instances with him, and I wanted to make sure he wasn't causing any problems over here."

"No, sir, he was just telling us where the finest places to stay in Waveland were," I said.

We all laughed awkwardly and went our separate ways. It wasn't twenty pedal strokes before I rode up beside Geoff and whispered, "Right on the beach."

We became hysterical, laughing until it was hard to breathe as we rode down the street, screaming at the tops of our lungs, "Right on the beach!" I would like to believe it was the Honey Bun and runner's high combination that sent us into hysterics, but in all honesty, we were losing our minds, and we didn't care. We knew we were free for just a bit longer, and we had become feral.

Floribama

We rode 211 miles over the next four days, complaining about consistent headwinds and how we didn't have enough metaphorical gas in the tank to ride farther each day. We were pushing hard, but honestly, we were tired and desperately wanted to be lazy. I dreamed of doing nothing except waking up, eating doughnuts, and binge-watching TV, but I wasn't there yet. I hadn't earned that privilege yet, so we kept riding. We made it to Alabama, stopping once to sleep, and by the next evening, we were already in Florida.

We rode through Pensacola quickly, riding over two bridges that looked like a great place to go fishing. After the bridges, we immediately hit Pensacola Beach and continued riding east along possibly the most beautiful and serene strip of beach I have ever seen.

Floribama

Riding down Florida Route 399 along the Gulf Islands National Seashore, we were surrounded by the bright white Pensacola sands on both sides of the road, the cove on our left, and the beach to our right. Barefoot beach-goers were everywhere, prancing across the street trying to escape the hot pavement. The sun was so bright it became a challenge to keep my eyes on the road with the incessant glare. Patches of grass covered the dunes, struggling to stay rooted in the fine silt-like sand. The entire ride along the national seashore, I wanted to slow down and enjoy the views. Our ride along the coast was coming to an end, and we would head inland soon, so I rode as slow as I could to take in the wonderment of it all. The sixty-two miles through Pensacola were not only a glimpse into a city where I would one day live, but a beautiful change of scenery that will forever be one of my favorite views of America.

The next day, we rode 149 miles to make up some of the time we had lost over the past four days. Luckily, we no longer had to deal with the Gulf Coast's constant headwinds. We had made it inland onto flat ground. Finally being able to ride fast, with little to no effort, felt incredible. It was as if the touring gods themselves were carrying me.

The long stretches of flat roads with absolutely no curves or bends in the road felt strange. I had to keep checking the map to make sure we hadn't missed our turn, because we never turned. Ever. There was one stretch on Route 20 where we went nearly seventy miles without turning, only hitting a few bends in the road here or there. No other state we rode through made roads that straight and long. I knew I had been touring too long when I started being opinionated about road planning.

We felt accomplished at the distance we covered in such a short amount of time and like we could do it again, day after day, until we crossed the finish line. We were confident we could finish ahead of schedule, as long as nothing unlucky happened. But of course, that wasn't in the cards.

We woke up early, as usual, and started riding through downtown Tallahassee. It was a beautiful city with some unexpected hills and a hidden, quaint charm that unfortunately seemed to be getting pushed out by commercial chains. Spanish moss enveloped the tall oak trees spread throughout the city and made it faintly resemble Charleston, while the rolling hills and traffic reminded me of where we had started biking, on the outskirts of Seattle.

I knew that something was wrong almost immediately. My face felt tingly and my breathing was sounding ragged, like a dull snore.

"Geoff, I'm not feeling too good, man!" I had to yell, trying to speak over the traffic. "My throat is feeling a bit itchy, and I think my lip is swelling up."

"You're fine, man. I don't see anything. Do you think you can make it a bit farther?" He was trying hard to beat the previous day's mileage.

"We're only fifteen miles into the day, and I'm for real not feeling too hot. Let's pull over somewhere and chill for a second."

I scanned the area, looking for anywhere to stop. I saw a fountain shooting out of a pond. Then I noticed the grass. Then the bench. *Park.*

"Pull into this park real quick. I've got to stop," I said, knowing I was having some kind of allergic reaction. As we pulled up next to the bench, it started to rain. *Sweet, when it rains, it pours.* Sitting down on the bench, I bent over to pull my rain jacket out of my pack. Blood rushed to my lips, making them pulse so hard they felt like they were about to burst.

"Geoff, are you sure my lips are OK?" I asked again.

This time he looked at me intently and his face couldn't hide his concern. "Whoa. You're not looking too good. Are you having an allergic reaction?"

"I don't know. I could be, but I have no idea from what," I said, but genuinely no clue from what. We didn't want to take any chances on letting it get any worse, so we went to a drugstore and got some allergy medication, just as my cheeks started swelling and my stomach became splotchy with hives. *Great.*

We got a hotel room five miles down the road, making the day's total mileage twenty. I was wracked with guilt for holding us back, especially since this wasn't the first time I had slowed us down. But I also didn't want to go anaphylactic in the middle of nowhere and start wheezing, struggling to breathe, and then get hit by a car. That wasn't how I had planned on ending the trip, so stopping for the day seemed like the best option. It was a real morale killer, but with just 180 miles or so left on the trip, we could make up the time.

We woke up, rode fifty-four miles to Madison, Florida, and slept. *I need to go farther.*

We woke up, rode eighty-two miles to Macclenny, Florida, and slept. *Solid day. Now I only have one day left, and I want it done before lunch.*

Finish Line

"I finally feel like I've found my place. And you know
what? It's right back where I started, but the difference is,
this time, I chose it."
– Z from the movie *Antz*

Sixty miles. We had sixty miles left until we saw the
Atlantic Ocean. All of the chronic soreness, heavyhearted
learning, and pedaling would be over before the sun went
down. I couldn't believe there would be no more surprise
lessons-to-be-learned on long, monotonous rides. I wouldn't
have to wake up and smell Geoff's odors. There would be no
more jaw-dropping scenic overlooks that made the entire
day's grueling ride worth it. Life was about to change forever in just sixty miles.

Finish Line

As we packed up and left the hotel, tears started to well up. *Damnit, Geoff, a bug flew in my eye; look somewhere else.* Nothing set the slight tears into motion; they just started falling. The only thing I could wrap my head around was realizing that I had finished the journey and that the trip had forever changed me. I was about to start a new life, free from the baggage I'd taken to Seattle. The zeal of life was taking over, and the realization of it all just broke me in the best of ways, making water fall from my face.

It was hard to breathe for the next sixty miles. I kept doing the pre-/post-cry stutter inhale. Kaitlyn always made fun of me for crying during movies since I never cried in real-life situations. The cellos and pianos playing during a dramatic heart-wrenching scene in a film make me emotional every time. She would be waiting for me at the hotel, and I needed to get all this emotion out before seeing her. She had supported me at the starting line in September, she'd known what was best for me when I wanted to quit in Arizona, and now she was waiting for me in Jacksonville, Florida, at the finish line. I needed to see her.

Pedal. Hard.

We pedaled as fast as we could that day, trying to navigate through Jacksonville's traffic. I kept thinking, "This is as far east as I can go."

Five thousand three hundred miles ago, I'd been a different person. I'd demanded growth from myself throughout the journey, and it had all started with letting

Hannah go, realizing that holding onto her wasn't allowing room for me to grow. I'd turned east at San Francisco, beginning my ride toward the man I wanted to be. I'd ridden through the echoing doubts from my dad, forgiving him for everything along the way. Now, here I was, as far east as I could go.

It was time to enter the next chapter of my life, and I would do it, knowing that I was free. I would do it, knowing that I had the perseverance to take on whatever challenges life threw my way.

Pedal. Hard.

I wish I could remember even a piece of Jacksonville, but the entire city was a blur. I slammed my feet into the pedals, time and again, until it felt like lactic acid was the only thing holding my legs together. I wanted it to hurt because I knew that pain meant I was going faster. *Faster. Go faster.* I would curse at every stoplight for making me stop, momentarily debating if I should just run the red light, with no regard for safety. A quick memory of the car crash in Washington erased any desire to blow through the red lights.

Before every track meet in high school, Geoff and I would psych each other out, often repeating to ourselves, "Leave it all on the track." Putting every ounce of energy into every race made the results, good or bad, something to be proud of. The last day of our trip had become like our final race of our senior year. We both knew that our cycle tour was ending in just a few short hours, so we pushed until our legs pulsed with pain, until our lungs felt like they were full of dust.

I didn't check to see how far we were from the finish. I knew we were close. I stayed focused on Geoff's rear tire, narrowly dodging all the debris, sand, and potholes. I was dodging a patch of sand when Geoff said, "There it is. There's our hotel."

We were done. The dream became a moment, which turned into 5,300 miles, and just like that, it was over.

We checked into the hotel, unloaded our gear, and set off to ride our bikes to the waves of the Atlantic Ocean. We carried our bikes up the stairs that led over the sand dunes. *God, I love not having my bags on this thing.* I rode across the bridge, entranced in the thick fog that made it impossible to see the crashing waves. I was staring so absent-mindedly that I nearly rode straight down the few stairs at the end of the bridge. I barely stopped in time, dismounted my bike, and remounted at the bottom of the stairs. The sand was impossibly difficult to ride through, but I pressed the pedals with every bit of strength I had. I wobbled a bit, then pushed harder to help regain balance. It felt like I had just summited Leggett again. I looked back to see how far I had traveled, lost my balance, and caught myself on the staircase. I had made it inches. I gave up on riding across the sand and carried my bike to the ocean.

With as much as I had battled the cold, it was appropriate to finish neck-deep, shivering in the salty sea. I held Janice over my head and carefully waded into the ocean. Holding my bike high above my head, getting smacked in the back by the freezing waves, I stood triumphant as on-lookers stared at me, no doubt wondering what I was doing. It was the only time I willingly and joyfully subjected myself to the cold on the entire trip. I asked Geoff if he had grabbed a good picture, and nearly ran out of the ocean. *That was fun, but now I need a shower for real.*

Since Geoff paid for the hotel, I let him shower first; then, I got whatever hot water I could coerce from the pipes. As I came out of the bathroom, making a joke about how the hotel was using the arctic water from the ocean for my shower, I turned to see Kaitlyn, running without reservation, straight toward me. She jumped into me, wrapping her arms and legs around me as though she hadn't seen me for years, crying as she said how proud she was. *I thought I had gotten all these tears out already.* I let them fall freely down my face. I had never been happier to see anyone in my life.

We rode our bikes for three months, two weeks, and one day. Now it was time for me to become the man I want-ed to be. Now it was time for my adventure to begin.

Three Months After

In the months following my adventure, I felt the best and worst feelings of my life. On the one hand, people would brag about my accomplishment and get me to tell stories to their friends, which I loved since telling stories is part of who I am. On top of that, I was proud of my accomplishment, but having so many people boast of what Geoff and I had done was humbling in a way I had never expected. I had no idea that riding a bicycle would touch so many lives the way it did. Even today, my dad still brags to his friends about it and tells me he's proud. It's tough to think that our relationship went from me internalizing a big "f*** you" on a mountain in the Sierra Nevadas to tears of reconciliation, all from riding a bicycle.

Three Months After

On the other hand, the far more painful hand, I went through what I call "the gray zone." It started about a month after the trip.

For weeks after the trip, I would try to sit and cuddle with Kaitlyn on the couch but couldn't sit still for longer than fifteen minutes. I don't mean my leg would bounce up and down either. I would have to get up and run three flights of stairs multiple times; only then could I sit back down. I had a weight set beside the couch, which I used throughout my "relaxing" time in the evenings. It drove Kaitlyn insane, but I could not stop moving. My body had become accustomed to converting food directly into blood sugar since I had had zero time to store any food as fat for months. Eat, move, repeat.

As much as I would have loved for that to continue, and for me to never net a positive amount of calories in a day, it didn't happen. I was tired of riding, moving, packing, and figuring out where to go. I desperately wanted to sit still. I willed myself into a catatonic state on the couch, and eventually, my body finally began storing fat. *I should have been careful what I wished for.*

One day Kaitlyn started laughing hysterically at the TV, and as I forced a smile, I realized that I hadn't felt emotion for weeks, not happy, sad, or angry, just nothing. I began paying attention to how I felt, and after about a week of that, I affectionately named the emptiness as "gray," the exact dull medium between black and white. Gray stuck with me for longer than I was comfortable with, so I went to the doctor to see if everything was ok. He immediately jumped into prescribing meds for a depressive state, but as I hopped off the table and started walking away, he asked about my calf tattoo. I had recently added a map of the United States around my bicycle sign. The second I told him that I had just gotten back a few weeks ago from a trip and had not touched a bicycle since, he withdrew the prescription, saying, "You're not depressed; you have what's known as the 'Post-Race Blues.'"

Excuse me, sir, what the effervescent hell are you talking about?

He told me that many endurance athletes experience a decrease in neurotransmitter production after completing their event, since most of the time, just like myself, they want nothing to do with training or exercise after the race. He went on to explain that during exercise, endorphins are released, which makes the body feel good... really good. It's why endurance athletes get injured as badly as they do, because they have all of those feel-good chemicals coursing through their bloodstream, which helps them ignore the pain, making the injury worse. So then, after months of training and producing all those endorphins, an endurance athlete's tolerance and stock levels are sky-high, but they've suddenly stopped exercising and are not making any more feel-good endorphins. Simple as that.

Three Months After

I went home and put up a stationary bike in front of the TV. I apparently had to wean myself off of my adventure.

Gear List

The following is a list of gear that both Geoff and I used on the trip. It is not all-encompassing, but when planning for my trip I did weeks of research to find all the necessary gear we would need. I don't go into brands too much, but try to stick to why the gear is useful or what to focus on when shopping.

On the Bike:

Bike - The Surley Long Haul Trucker - This bike earned the nickname "Janice" because she is slow and heavy. However, I chose the Long Haul Trucker (LHT) because it's made of steel, which is likely to be easily repaired by anyone who can weld. It also has every braze-on that any cycle tourist needs. This bike was highly regarded as the gold-standard for long distance touring in 2012.

Bike specific multi-tool - There are 100's of models out there, so don't overthink it. Just make sure it has the proper size hex key, the right sized spoke wrench, and a flat/phillips screwdriver.

Burley bike trailer - As mentioned in my story, cycle touring with a trailer is hard, and I'm likely to never tour with one again. However, as far as trailers are concerned, the Burley was probably the best out there. It was durable, spacious, and lightweight.

Cycling clothes - North Face was Geoff's brand of choice because it's what was sold at the bike shop he worked at. But I'll break this category down a little bit more:

> Jersey - I've used jersey's from every price point, and it's going to come down to comfort around the arm, armpit, and length. Make sure it's not rubbing anywhere and it's long enough to cover your butt crack. *There's nothing more embarrassing than showing your ass.*

> Chamois shorts - I know I said panniers were my second most important piece of gear, but this is a close, close competitor. Make sure the chamois is comfortable, and the seams don't rub anywhere. I wore my shorts for three months straight, so comfort

was key.

Socks - Cycling companies make bike-specific socks for a reason; they are more comfortable. Does it make a huge difference in my opinion, no. But Geoff would argue differently. I used white, Hanes cotton socks. Just make sure they are cotton and don't overthink it.

Cycling shoes - I used a pair of insanely cheap Shimano commuter shoes with SPD cleats. They were cloth, with black laces and I still use them, 10 years later. Geoff used a pair of Specialized road bike shoes with SPD cleats. I chose to get commuter shoes so I could get off the bike and immediately walk around and start setting up camp, or go inside a restaurant to get something to eat.

Helmet - No one looks cool in a helmet, so don't worry about it. Just wear one!

Mini-pump (manual) - We decided to use a manual pump, as opposed to a CO_2 inflator, because we didn't want to carry the extra cartridges. Also, looking back, if we only had a CO_2 inflator, we would have run out of gas, more than once, while in the desert.

Niterider bike light - A phenomenal bike light. However, I don't use bike lights anymore. I invested in a headlamp for running at night, and now use it when I ride. A bike mounted light only faces one direction, and that's not always where I need to look. The headlamp fixes that and it's very comfortable. Make sure to get one with the band that goes over the top of the head and not just around it. That band keeps the lamp from falling down my forehead and saves me a ton of frustration.

Panniers - I used a set of red canvas Nashbar Panniers (2011/12 model). On a budget, and eager to start my tour, this was the best I could afford. Looking back, I would not have tried to save money on my panniers. They were, aside from my bike, my most crucial pieces of equipment. There are waterproof panniers that lock onto the rack, and are much more spacious and easily organized. Do not settle for cheap panniers, unless that's all you can afford. In which case, go tour and have fun!

Repair kit - I can't stress this one enough. Make sure to have enough patches and glue to fix 20 flats. Remember though, pine tree sap can be used to supplement glue in a pinch.

Extra tubes - Two tubes per tire *should* be good.

Specialized water bottles - Make sure to have enough water on the bike to ride another three to five hours, at all times. We ran out of water more than once, and it never ended well.

Off the Bike:

Bungees - My shoddy and derelict panniers would never have made it cross country without many, many bungee cords. Bungees are not a necessity, until they are.

Extra clothes and shoes - Take two t-shirts, one pair of athletic shorts, and one pair of regular shorts for off the bike. Wearing the bike kit all day is fine, until you're walking around camp, sitting by a fire, etc. and just want to relax. Off-the-bike-clothes will make a huge difference.

Food - There are grocery stores in most places in America. Don't overpack. Just buy a day or two at a time.

Cookware - We had small, foldable bowls with accompanying collapsable silverware. Don't bring too much, and make sure it's easily cleanable and foldable.

Hammock - Not necessary. It's a cool novelty item, but was useless in the desert and in the Redwood Forest. Also, they get really cold if you do not use a sleep-pad with them too.

Knife - Geoff carried a three inch pocket knife on the trip, which came in handy a lot while camping. I'll be sure to take a small one next time.

Pillow - As my one creature comfort, I brought my orthopedic pillow from home. It was a large, cumbersome mess with my pillowcase flapping around behind me on the bike, but I didn't care. I was willing to deal with it if it meant a good night's sleep. *Do what you want. It's your tour.*

Sleeping bag - I used a cheap bag that was just fancy enough to come with a stuff-sack. I will never skimp on a good sleeping bag again. However, I won't use down either, because my bag got wet on more than one occasion, and once down gets wet it will not insulate at all.

Sleep pad - Whether foam, blow-up, or otherwise, any one who has slept on the ground will agree, it's a must-have! I used a blow-up sleep pad from REI. I was hesitant at first because I was afraid of it popping, but I had enough glue and patches from my bike repair kit to fix it, so figured it would all work out. Luckily it did.

Stove - We used a JetBoil camping stove, and I couldn't have been happier. It brought the water to a boil insanely fast. It's great for rice and beans, soup, oatmeal, etc. **Make sure to have enough propane gas**

Tarp - We got a $20 tarp from REI and it worked great. It proved useful everyday and I will never go camping without one.

Tent - As I talked about during the tour stories, we used a small, two-person tent and it worked well. After the trip, I bought a lightweight Big Agnes tent, and I love it. After I saw Jessie using it in Oregon, I had to have one. It's the best backpacking/cycle touring tent I've ever seen.

Thank You

Amber, Chase, Cameron, & Simms for being the best of friends during a time when I needed it most. I wouldn't be where I am without each of you.

Ashley and Dave for being our first hosts and letting us get ready for a trip that changed our lives. Your generosity set the tone for the trip and I will never forget it.

Ben for your blood and sweat. Your willingness to keep showing up to help is astounding.

Brian Carter for your unbreakable loyalty. We've survived more jeopardizing situations than I care to recall, yet we still keep showing up. Thanks for the night's we'll never remember, with the friends we will never forget.

Thank You

Cameron Segars for the roaring laughs at the same lunch table that Geoff and I decided to ride across America.

Chasen Callahan for being a mentor when I needed direction.

Clayton Anderson for reminding me that the adventure has yet to come.

Cody Hartman for being a founding member of the breakfast club. Thank you for always showing up and helping me brainstorm new ways for self-improvement.

Dad and Carla for not making life easy. I've always learned the hard way and needed someone to push-back. Thanks for meeting me half-way.

Dakota Morrison for always thinking I was a superhero, even when I was a complete ass. I'm proud to be your big brother.

Fawn Campbell for creating your incredible daughter. I promise I will keep trying to impress her and make her laugh.

Geoffrey Buell for all the unforgettable years spent together, learning how to make each other stronger, faster, better people. You've helped me thoroughly test my boundaries and break them. I wouldn't want my story of cycling across America to be any different, and I couldn't have done it without you. Thanks for everything, and I still owe you one long-ass walk.

George for giving one of my best friends someone to grow old with.

Kaitlyn Morrison for pushing me to be a better person, even when I fight back. I never would have finished the bike ride, much less the book, without your support. I owe you more than I can comprehend. I love you, forever.

Leon for besting me in every competition. You are truly my superior. However, in preparation for my comeback, I might haphazardly train for at least a few days before the holidays every year. May the best man pay for drinks.

Mom and Troy for supporting me from day one of this venture. You let your little boy ride his bike across America and become a man his own way. Thank you.

Oma and Grandaddy for teaching me consistency and hardwork. I love both of you, dearly.

Quinn Guilds for being my Pensacola Life-Partner. I still think back fondly.

Reid McGahey for all of the fire-melon, crate-boarding, house jumping, firework smoke-stained, wigwam building, barefoot 10K, copper for Subway days. You taught me how to handle fear... and possibly broke my adrenal gland in the process. But without our stunts, I never would have had the guts to ride across America. Thank you.

Ryan Langford for being a leader to all of us new guys. Your

Thank You

gruff and salty attitude is a beautiful coverup for that tender heart, you 'ol bastard.

Sabrina Rodriguez for supporting me in a way only you could. You were a steady friend in my time of chaos.

Sela Ballard for keeping things in perspective when we were young. Your grit and determination motivates me everyday. I'm proud to be your big brother.

Stephen Edens for always finding ways to contribute, help, and better my family's life.

Steven and Karen McGahey for not kicking me out of your house too often. Y'all were a home away from home, and I'm forever grateful for it.

Tyler Gulovsen for helping me survive one of the hardest, funnest times of my life. The lessons I learned as a part of SNRP1 will forever stay with me.

William Smart for teaching leadership lessons, even when you thought no one was looking. Also, for coffee roulette.

Yaris for an unforgettable moment in Nevada. Your willingness to re-ride that mountain for a soak in a hot spring still inspires me.

I would also like to thank the people below for making this book possible:

Whether we've shared years together, or are complete strangers, without you, this story would still be an idea, floating around in my head. Your support means more to me than I can put into words.

Adam Schroeder

Alexis Broome Roy

Barry and Reba Edens

Benjamin Lynch

Brent D Armstrong

Caitlin Martin Cothran

Cameron B. Cochran

Charles B. Jennings (C.B.)

Charles Swearington

Christian Perkins

David J.

Devin Okelly

Thank You

Dillon Porter

Jacob Hagan

James C. Devno

James Cavanaugh

Jaryd Peppmuller

Jeff Spencer

Jennifer

Jim Ryan

Joanna Lyttle

Josh Moffitt

Josh Williams

Justine Chasmar Stauffer

Kayleen Freeborn

Kevin Satterfield

King

Marcin Spoczynski

Tour Stories

Mark Pinto

Matt Klaver

Matt Parris

Morgan Dawson

Pam Kirby

Philips Family

Rebekah Ann Rodriguez

Sam

Sesley McDonald

Viviana

Wendie

www.ingramcontent.com/pod-product-compliance
Lightning Source LLC
Chambersburg PA
CBHW061817040426
42447CB00012B/2696